Bal's SPICE KITCHEN

Bal Arneson

whitecap

EDITORS: Theresa Best, Jesse Marchand and Elizabeth McLean
DESIGN: Michelle Furbacher
COVER DESIGN: Andrew Bagatella
FOOD PHOTOGRAPHY: Tracey Kusiewicz
ADDITIONAL PHOTOGRAPHY: Michelle Furbacher (inset, pages 1, 25, 29, 38, 66, 93, 97, 156; red chili flakes, page 8; saffron, page 9); olgakr/iStock/Thinkstock (bay leaves, page 6); Eva Gruendemann/iStock/Thinkstock (garam masala, page 8); barol16/iStock/Thinkstock (mustard seeds, page 8); iStockphoto.com/marylooo (oregano, page 8); iStockphoto.com/CamiloTorres (tamarind, page 9); Cathy Yeulet/Hemera/Thinkstock (tandoori masala, page 9); iStockphoto.com/grafvision (inset, page 52)
FOOD STYLING: Bal Arneson and Tracey Kusiewicz
PROOFREADING: Lesley Cameron

Printed in Canada by Friesens

Library and Archives Canada Cataloguing in Publication

Arneson, Bal, 1972–, author
     Bal's spice kitchen / Bal Arneson.
Includes index.
ISBN 978-1-77050-195-9 (pbk.)
     1. Spices. 2. Cooking (Spices). 3. Cookbooks. I. Title.
TX406.A76 2013   641.3'383   C2013-904203-2

The publisher acknowledges the financial support of the Government of Canada through the Canada Book Fund (CBF) and the Province of British Columbia through the Book Publishing Tax Credit.

14 15 16 17 18   5 4 3 2 1

As a mother I am blessed.
My inspiration for this book came from my
two amazing kids, Anoop and Aaron.

contents

Introduction

Memories of my mom teaching me how to cook by the village barbecue pit when I was a little girl in India are still very close to my heart. While other kids would run around and play tag, I would sit with my mother as she taught me how to grasp an onion in my little hands in order to carefully slice it. We didn't have any cutting boards, so all the chopping was done on our hands.

She would hum songs while preparing the food and I would always ask her what song she was singing. She would always reply, "It's an old song, you won't know," and then continue to perfectly chop the seasonal vegetables. Every single dish she cooked was mouth-watering, and the neighbourhood women and kids would come by to get a taste of her food. I not only learned how to cook, I also learned how to cook passionately, injecting a lot of love into the food when we couldn't afford many ingredients.

My journey as a cook, author and TV host began when, after coming to Canada via an arranged marriage, the circumstances of my life changed. I found myself alone with my young daughter and needed a source of income. My village cooking skills came to my rescue and I started catering and giving cooking classes. After eating my food, people always asked me if I had a cookbook. That is what inspired me to write my first cookbook, *Everyday Indian*. Indian food is often thought of as heavy and creamy, and people were amazed by how healthy and delicious my food was. I followed up my first book with *Bal's Quick & Healthy Indian*, which focused on preparing quick yet flavourful Indian meals.

The idea behind *Bal's Spice Kitchen* was to provide recipes for all-round favourite dishes complemented by new spice combinations. I wanted to create quick and healthy meals that are still mouth-wateringly delicious, meals that both a novice cook and a professional chef would enjoy making. When I shared my banana split recipe with chef Bobby Flay, his first response was, "I have never thought of that technique before. I'm going to use it in my restaurant." A common comment I read in emails from across North America is, "Bal, spices used to be such a mystery for us and Indian food always looked so complicated, so thank you for making it not intimidating. Now I have the confidence to cook food with spices for my family."

I often tell people: Follow your palate. If you like floral flavours, add green cardamoms. If you like heat, add more ginger and paprika. If you like citrus, add coriander seeds or ground coriander. If you like comforting, warm, earthy flavours, try my garam masala or add more cumin to your dishes. Make your own curry using the spices and flavours you enjoy.

My passion for food and wanting to share my recipes is the reason I am here today writing this book. These recipes reflect my travels around North America, to Paris and other parts of Europe, as well as my newly developed palate from judging on the shows *Iron Chef America* and *Bobby's Dinner Battle*, with Bobby Flay. It is a blessing to be on this journey and an honour to share my recipes with you.

My wish: No child should ever go to bed hungry. When I was growing up, on many nights there wasn't enough food to fill my stomach.

My daughter and I have designed a piece of jewelry that symbolizes my wish: The spoon-and-fork necklace I am wearing in the photograph. A portion of the proceeds from sales of the necklace will go to charities that feed the hungry. Visit balarneson.com for more information.

Indian
seasonings &
spice blends

Glossary of Seasonings

 BAY LEAVES are highly aromatic, with a distinctive flavour. They are usually used dried, as they have a bitter taste when fresh. They are not used on their own in Indian cooking, but are a common ingredient in the garam masala spice blend.

 CARDAMOM grows in pods that contain seeds, and comes in three varieties: green, which is considered the best; white, which is just green but bleached; and brown, which is not considered true cardamom. Its warm, slightly peppery flavour is often used in sweets but can also be used in savoury dishes. Recipes may call for whole pods or only the seeds, or for ground cardamom. I like the bite of the seeds, but some may find their texture too rough and ground cardamom will give the same flavour. If you cook with pods, be sure to remove them before serving.

 CINNAMON is the inner bark of an evergreen tree. It is available in either stick or ground form and works nicely in both sweet and savoury dishes. Its flavour is fragrant and sweet, with a warm taste.

 CLOVES are the unopened buds of an evergreen tree. They have a pungent flavour that can be overwhelming, so this spice is used in moderation in both savoury and sweet dishes.

 CORIANDER (also known as cilantro) comes from the fruit of the coriander plant. It has a mild, sweet taste with a clear hint of orange peel. It is used in sweet and savoury dishes and is an essential ingredient in curry powder.

Glossary of Seasonings (*continued*)

 CUMIN is part of the parsley family and can be purchased in seed or ground form. It has a subtle, warm, earthy flavour that goes well with fish, vegetables and grains.

 CURRY LEAVES (unrelated to curry powder) can be purchased fresh, frozen or dried. Their flavour is a bit like that of a mild curry powder. Fresh leaves have a much stronger flavour than dried, so use fresh when you can. If you use dried, use the same amount as fresh.

 FENNEL SEEDS, from the fennel plant, are available as whole seeds and in ground form. Anise-flavoured, they have a warm and fragrant taste and complement meat, vegetables and fish nicely.

 FENUGREEK comes in leaf and seed form. It has a strong aroma and a bitter taste when uncooked. Dry-roasting mellows the flavour of the seeds. It is an essential spice in many Indian dishes and spice mixtures.

 GARAM MASALA is the primary spice blend of North Indian cooking. There are as many versions as there are cooks. A basic garam masala always includes cumin, coriander, cardamom, peppercorns and cloves; other spices can be added according to the dish. (See my recipe on page 11.)

 MUSTARD SEEDS come in three varieties: black seeds have a pungent flavour; brown are slightly bitter; and white have an initial sickly sweetness followed by mild heat. Brown seeds are the ones most commonly used in Indian cooking.

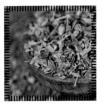 OREGANO is an aromatic leaf commonly used in Mediterranean cuisine. In fresh or dried form, it is typically added toward the end of the cooking process because heat will cause it to lose its flavour. It is a great savoury flavouring.

 RED CHILI FLAKES are dried, red-hot chili peppers that have been broken into pieces. They are a quick way to add instant flavour and texture to a bland dish.

 SAFFRON is collected from the crocus flower. It has a warm, spicy, very potent flavour, and infuses whatever it touches with a distinct golden hue that can't be duplicated. It is typically added to sauces, soups, fish and rice dishes.

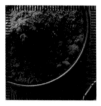 SMOKED PAPRIKA has a deep red colour and a strong smoky flavour. It provides very little heat but gives a lovely red colour to dishes, and goes well with both meats and vegetables.

 STAR ANISE is a seed shaped like a star, with a strong smell of anise mixed with licorice. The flavour is similar to anise but stronger, with a more pronounced licorice taste. It is ideal for flavouring chicken, fish and clear soups.

 TAMARIND comes from the curved, reddish brown pod of the tamarind tree. It is generally sold in a highly concentrated chunk, which can be used in many ways. It has a sweet-sour, fruity aroma and taste that work nicely with fish and poultry dishes.

 TANDOORI MASALA is a spice blend traditionally for use in a clay oven, and is very important in Indian cooking. The ingredients can vary between regions but the rich, smoky flavour base is the same everywhere. (See my recipe on page 11.)

 TURMERIC is the underground root of a perennial. It has a pungent, bitter, musky flavour and adds a beautiful orange-yellow colour to food. It is essential in curry powder and an important flavouring for all Indian cooking.

Blended Indian spices are called masala. I always love mixing different spices together to make unique blends to give to my friends for birthdays or other celebrations so that they can use them in their everyday cooking too. I would like to share a few of my blends with you. The best way to store these spices is to keep them in an airtight jar in a cool, dark place to keep the flavours in for a long time.

Spice Blends

Steak Masala

2 Tbsp (30 mL) cumin seeds

1 Tbsp (15 mL) fennel seeds

1 tsp (5 mL) brown mustard seeds

1 tsp (5 mL) black peppercorns

¼ cup (60 mL) fenugreek leaves

1 tsp (5 mL) smoked paprika

½ tsp (2 mL) red chili flakes

½ tsp (2 mL) salt

In a skillet, toast the cumin seeds, fennel seeds, mustard seeds and peppercorns on medium-low heat until the spice aromas fill the air, about 30 seconds. Turn off the heat and let the pan cool.

Process the spices in a spice grinder until coarsely ground, then add the fenugreek leaves, paprika, chili flakes and salt and give the grinder a quick spin.

Makes about ⅓ cup (80 mL).

Store in an airtight jar in a cool, dark place for up to 3 months.

Seafood Masala

1 Tbsp (15 mL) mixed peppercorns

8 whole star anise

2 Tbsp (30 mL) coriander seeds

1 tsp (5 mL) whole cloves

1 tsp (5 mL) fennel seeds

1 tsp (5 mL) ground cinnamon

Toast the peppercorns in a hot skillet for about 1 minute, until they are aromatic.

In a spice grinder, process the peppercorns, star anise, coriander seeds, cloves and fennel seeds into powder. Add the cinnamon and process for a few seconds to combine.

Makes about ¼ cup (60 mL).

Store in an airtight jar in a cool, dark place for up to 3 months.

Garam Masala

12 whole cloves

8 green cardamom pods

6 black cardamom pods

6 bay leaves

4-inch (10 cm) cinnamon stick

2 Tbsp (30 mL) coriander seeds

2 Tbsp (30 mL) cumin seeds

1 tsp (5 mL) black peppercorns

1 tsp (5 mL) mustard seeds

In a skillet, toast all the spices over low heat, stirring frequently. When gorgeous aromas start coming out of the skillet, about 30 seconds, turn off the heat and let the pan cool.

Makes about ⅓ cup (80 mL).

Process the spices in a spice grinder. Store in an airtight jar in a cool, dark place for up to 3 months.

Tandoori Masala

5 Tbsp (75 mL) smoked paprika

1 Tbsp (15 mL) garam masala

1 tsp (5 mL) ground turmeric

1 tsp (5 mL) garlic powder

1 tsp (5 mL) ground ginger

¼ tsp (1 mL) salt

¼ tsp (1 mL) ground cloves

¼ tsp (1 mL) ground nutmeg

Put all the ingredients in a small, airtight jar and shake to blend well. Add to yogurt to make a marinade for chicken or fish.

Makes about ⅓ cup (80 mL).

Store in an airtight jar in a cool, dark place for up to 3 months.

Spice Blends *(continued)*

Spicy Curry Masala

2 Tbsp (30 mL) ground mango*

2 Tbsp (30 mL) ground pomegranate*

2 Tbsp (30 mL) garam masala

2 Tbsp (30 mL) fenugreek leaves

1 Tbsp (15 mL) ground black pepper

1 tsp (5 mL) ground turmeric

1 tsp (5 mL) red chili powder

½ tsp (2 mL) salt

Put all the ingredients in a small, airtight jar and shake to blend well. Store in a cool, dark place.

Makes about ½ cup (125 mL).

Store in an airtight jar in a cool, dark place for up to 3 months.

* Ground mango and ground pomegranate are available in Asian grocery stores.

Mild Curry Masala

1 Tbsp (15 mL) garam masala

1 tsp (5 mL) ground turmeric

1 tsp (5 mL) ground fennel

1 tsp (5 mL) ground cardamom

½ tsp (2 mL) ground cinnamon

¼ tsp (1 mL) black pepper

¼ tsp (1 mL) salt

Put all the ingredients in a small, airtight jar and shake to blend well.

Makes about 2 to 3 Tbsp.

Store in an airtight container in a cool, dark place for up to 3 months.

soups

Mango and Cardamom Soup / 16

Bitter Melon and Coconut Soup / 18

Cumin, Coriander and Tomato Soup / 19

Spinach and Asparagus Soup with
Parmesan / 20

Kale and Green Pea Soup / 22

Rapini and Paneer Soup / 23

Bell Pepper and Curried Avocado
Soup / 24

Coriander Squash Soup / 25

Yam and Avocado Soup / 26

Four Mushroom and Turnip Soup / 27

Roasted Corn Chowder with Cardamom
and Fenugreek / 28

Cold Yogurt Soup with Fennel, Basil
and Pine Nuts / 29

Mixed Lentils with Leek Soup / 30

Fennel and Black Bean Soup / 31

Mussels and Curry Leaf Soup / 32

Shredded Chicken and Sage Soup / 33

Beefy Vegetable Soup with Fresh
Herbs / 34

All my friends and family members know how much I love mangoes. I try to incorporate them into everything I cook. I only eat mangoes in season because during the rest of the year they have no flavour. I also enjoy playing with the flavours of cardamom. Their floral flavour goes well with the sweetness of mango.

Mango and Cardamom Soup

1 Tbsp (15 mL) grapeseed oil

1 tsp (5 mL) finely chopped ginger

¼ tsp (1 mL) red chili flakes

1 cup (250 mL) vegetable broth

1 tsp (5 mL) ground cardamom

salt and pepper to taste

4 medium ripe mangoes, peeled and pitted

thinly sliced basil leaves for garnish

In a large saucepan, cook the oil, ginger and chili flakes on medium heat for 30 seconds. Add the broth, cardamom, salt and pepper then the mangoes and bring the mixture to a boil. Turn the heat off and let cool. Purée in a food processor.

Reheat the soup before serving. To serve, garnish each bowl with basil leaves. **SERVES 4 TO 6**

SUGGESTED WINE

2007 Sette Coppa by D'Angelo Estate Winery

MANGO AND CARDAMOM SOUP (BOTTOM), CUMIN, CORIANDER AND TOMATO SOUP (PAGE 19) (TOP)

Even 20 years ago, when I was in India, type 2 diabetes was beginning to rise in the population, and it was always said that bitter melon has the health benefit of reducing your blood sugar. Bitter melon is a very acquired taste and not everyone likes its bitter flavour. I grew up eating them, so for me it's a perfect food. The addition of coconut milk here helps to reduce the bitterness of the melon. Floral flavours from the cardamom and licorice from the fennel seeds make a great spice combination.

Bitter Melon and Coconut Soup

2 Tbsp (30 mL) grapeseed oil

1 Tbsp (15 mL) thinly sliced ginger

1 Tbsp (15 mL) thinly sliced garlic

1 Tbsp (15 mL) fennel seeds

1 tsp (5 mL) cardamom seeds

salt and pepper to taste

8 bitter melons, seeds removed, chopped

2 potatoes, peeled and cubed

3 cups (750 mL) vegetable broth

14 oz (398 mL) can coconut milk

In a large saucepan, combine the oil, ginger, garlic, fennel seeds, cardamom seeds, salt, pepper, bitter melons and potatoes. Cook on medium-high for 2 minutes, stirring frequently. Add the broth and bring to a boil, then turn down the heat to medium-low and cook until the potatoes are tender, 15 to 20 minutes.

Add the coconut milk and cook for 5 minutes. Turn off the heat and let the mixture cool. Purée in a food processor.

Reheat the soup before serving. **SERVES 4 TO 6**

The aroma of the coriander and garam masala nicely complements the sweet flavour of the ginger. This is a perfect soup for all seasons.

Cumin, Coriander and Tomato Soup

5 cups (1.25 L) cherry tomatoes, halved

4 Tbsp (60 mL) grapeseed oil

1 Tbsp (15 mL) cumin seeds

1 Tbsp (15 mL) coriander seeds

1 tsp (5 mL) garam masala (see page 11)

1 medium onion, chopped

6 garlic cloves, peeled

salt and pepper to taste

2 cups (500 mL) vegetable broth

2 Tbsp thinly sliced ginger

Preheat the oven to 375°F (190°C). On a baking tray, lay out the tomatoes and sprinkle with 2 Tbsp (30 mL) of the oil, the cumin seeds, coriander seeds, garam masala, onion, garlic, salt and pepper. Bake for 30 minutes.

Remove the tray and let cool slightly. Scrape the tomatoes and spices into a blender. Add the broth and purée.

In a large saucepan, heat the remaining 2 Tbsp (30 mL) oil and cook the ginger on medium-high until it turns brown, about 30 seconds.

Reheat the soup before serving. Drop a few pieces of ginger overtop each serving. **SERVES 4 TO 6**

Pictured on page 17.

This green magic potion is the best thing you will ever eat. Not only is it tasty and very healthy, it is also quick to make. A sprinkle of cheese on top and the presentation is elegant too.

Spinach and Asparagus Soup with Parmesan

2 Tbsp (30 mL) grapeseed oil

1 medium onion, chopped

1 Tbsp (15 mL) chopped ginger

1 Tbsp (15 mL) garam masala (see page 11)

1 lb (500 g) white asparagus, hard ends removed, cut into 1-inch (2.5 cm) pieces

2 cups (500 mL) frozen spinach, chopped

5 cups (1.25 L) vegetable broth

½ cup (125 mL) white wine

1 Tbsp (15 mL) oregano

salt and pepper to taste

¼ cup (60 mL) fresh grated Parmesan cheese

In a large pot, heat the oil and cook the onion and ginger on medium-high for 3 minutes, until the onion is tender.

Add the garam masala and asparagus. Turn the heat to medium-low and cook, stirring frequently, until the asparagus is tender, about 6 to 8 minutes. Add the rest of the ingredients except the Parmesan cheese and let the soup simmer for 3 to 5 minutes.

To serve, sprinkle each bowl of soup with Parmesan.

SERVES 4

SUGGESTED WINE
2011 Rosé by Upper Bench Estate Winery

I make traditional soups, but sometimes I like to push the boundaries of my kids' palates and create soups like this. It's not often that you find something that is very healthy and very flavourful, but this recipe has that magic. Kale is not only low in calories, it is also high in iron and a great source of fibre.

Kale and Green Pea Soup

2 Tbsp (30 mL) grapeseed oil

1 Tbsp (15 mL) chopped garlic

1 Tbsp (15 mL) ground coriander

1 tsp (5 mL) ground cumin

¼ tsp (1 mL) ground cloves

salt and pepper to taste

4 cups (1 L) chopped kale

2 cups (500 mL) vegetable broth

1 cup (250 mL) frozen peas

In a large pot, heat the oil and cook the garlic, coriander, cumin, cloves, salt and pepper on medium-high for 2 minutes, stirring frequently. Add the kale, broth and peas and bring to a boil. Turn the heat to low and let it simmer, uncovered, for 3 to 5 minutes, until the kale is tender and the peas are cooked. **SERVES 4**

Sag, sometimes spelled saag, is an Indian dish made with rapini and spinach that both of my kids enjoy. When I was growing up in India, I would look forward to winter because that meant fresh rapini in the garden. My mother would show me how to pick each rapini from the dirt and tear the leaves before finely chopping the stem. She made the best rapini stew in the village, and I could literally lick my bowl. This recipe takes me back to my childhood days. It is simple and quick to make. I use paneer, which is Indian cheese, but you could use crumbled feta instead.

Rapini and Paneer Soup

2 Tbsp (30 mL) grapeseed oil

2 Tbsp (30 mL) garlic, finely chopped

1 Tbsp (15 mL) finely chopped ginger

salt and pepper to taste

1 small green chili, chopped (keep the seeds if you like the heat)

4 cups (1 L) vegetable broth

10 cups (2.5 L) chopped rapini

1 cup (250 mL) crumbled paneer (see page 51)

In a large pot, heat the oil and cook the garlic and ginger on medium-high for 3 minutes, until the ginger is fully cooked. Add the salt, pepper and green chili then the broth and rapini and cook over medium-low, uncovered, until the rapini is tender, 8 to 10 minutes. Turn off the heat and let the mixture cool.

Purée in a food processor. Add the paneer to the soup and reheat before serving. **SERVES 4 TO 6**

When I discovered bell peppers, I soon started eating them raw as a healthy snack. What I love about them is that when they are grilled, they have a sweet candy flavour. When you add caramelized onions, the nutty flavour of avocado and my spices, this becomes a very lovely and soothing creation.

Bell Pepper and Curried Avocado Soup

4 Tbsp (60 mL) grapeseed oil

1 Tbsp (15 mL) ground cumin

1 tsp (5 mL) smoked paprika

salt and pepper to taste

6 red bell peppers

4 yellow bell peppers

1½ cups (375 mL) vegetable broth

1 Tbsp (15 mL) chopped garlic

1 medium onion, chopped

¼ cup (60 mL) loosely packed fresh curry leaves

1 medium-hard avocado, peeled, pitted and cubed

Preheat the oven to 350°F (175°C). In a small bowl, combine 2 Tbsp (30 mL) of the oil, the ground cumin, paprika, salt and pepper and mix well.

Cut the peppers into quarters. Discard the seeds and place the peppers on a baking sheet. Brush the spiced oil on the peppers and bake until partly done, 20 to 30 minutes. Let the peppers cool, then purée in a blender with the vegetable broth.

In a skillet, heat the remaining 2 Tbsp (30 mL) oil and cook the garlic and onion on medium-high, stirring frequently, until the onion is tender, about 5 minutes. Add the curry leaves and cook for another minute. Add the avocado and cook for 30 seconds, still stirring.

To serve, heat the pepper purée, stirring frequently, and pour an equal amount into 4 shallow bowls. Dollop a heaping spoonful of the avocado mixture on top of each bowl. **SERVES 4**

When I was growing up in the village, squash was only used to make this thick soup with potatoes. I can still taste the juicy flavours and remember eating the soup without any roti or rice. This recipe is very quick, healthy and easy to make. It freezes well too—not that there is any left to freeze in my kitchen.

Coriander Squash Soup

2 Tbsp (30 mL) grapeseed oil

2 onions, chopped

1 Tbsp (15 mL) chopped ginger

1 tsp (5 mL) cumin seeds

1 tsp (5 mL) coriander seeds

1 tsp (5 mL) garam masala
(see page 11)

salt and pepper to taste

4 cups (1 L) vegetable stock

1 small carrot, chopped

1 potato, chopped

1 medium butternut squash,
diced

In a large pot on medium-high, heat the oil and cook the onion, ginger, cumin seeds, coriander seeds, garam masala, salt and pepper for 3 to 4 minutes, stirring frequently, until the onions are tender.

Add the stock, carrot, potato and squash. Bring to a boil, reduce the heat to medium-low and cook, uncovered, until the potatoes and squash are tender, about 20 to 30 minutes. Turn off the heat.

Let the mixture cool, then purée in a food processor. Reheat the soup and serve warm. **SERVES 4 TO 6**

I believe that food should not only taste delicious but also look beautiful. Here, I have tried to achieve that by combining the natural colours of avocado and yams. The cardamom has a nice floral flavour, which goes well with the nutty taste of fresh avocado. I have not added any flavours to the yam purée because it has a very sweet natural flavour that complements the aromas of the spices.

Yam and Avocado Soup

2 medium yams, peeled and cubed

2 Tbsp (30 mL) grapeseed oil

2 Tbsp (30 mL) thinly sliced ginger

1 tsp (5 mL) cumin seeds

½ tsp (2 mL) brown mustard seeds

¼ cup (60 mL) loosely packed fresh curry leaves

¼ tsp (1 mL) salt

1 large avocado, peeled and pitted

1 tsp (5 mL) ground cardamom

In a saucepan, place the cubed yams in enough water to cover them. Bring the water to a boil, then reduce the heat to low and simmer, uncovered, until the yams are fully cooked, about 12 to 15 minutes. Let the mixture cool and purée in a food processor. Add more water if needed for a smooth consistency. Put the purée back in the saucepan and keep it warm.

While the yams are cooking, prepare the spice mixture. In a skillet, heat the oil and cook the ginger on medium heat for 2 minutes, stirring frequently. Add the cumin seeds, mustard seeds, curry leaves and salt and cook for 1 minute. Turn off the heat.

In a large, deep bowl, blend the avocado, cardamom and ½ cup (125 mL) water with an electric mixer until it turns into a smooth, thick liquid.

To serve, spoon the avocado soup into serving bowls. Top with 1 cup (250 mL) of the yam purée and 1 Tbsp (15 mL) of the spice mixture. **SERVES 4 TO 6**

Mushrooms have an earthy and nutty flavour that I love, and if I could, I would use them in every dish. I added turnip to this soup because I eat turnips like apples. They have a nice sharp taste that works very well with the mushrooms, especially when the aromatic flavours of the spices are added.

Four Mushroom and Turnip Soup

2 Tbsp (30 mL) grapeseed oil

1 medium onion, chopped

1 Tbsp (15 mL) ground cumin

1 tsp (5 mL) brown mustard seeds

¼ tsp (1 mL) ground cloves

¼ tsp (1 mL) red chili flakes

¼ cup (60 mL) loosely packed fresh curry leaves

salt and pepper to taste

4 cups (1 L) mixed mushrooms, chopped (button, portobello, shiitake and oyster)

4 cups (1 L) vegetable broth

1 cup (250 mL) grated turnip

½ cup (125 mL) finely chopped green onions

In a large pot, heat the oil and cook the onion, cumin, mustard seeds, cloves, chili flakes, curry leaves, salt and pepper on medium-high for 2 minutes, stirring frequently. Add the mushrooms and cook for 7 to 9 minutes, stirring frequently, until the mushrooms are almost cooked.

Add the broth, turnip and green onions and cook for 3 to 5 minutes, until the turnip is just tender. **SERVES 4 TO 6**

The only way I ate corn growing up was when my mother roasted it on the coals. As it cooked, the sugar in the corn would attain a very sweet, caramelized nutty flavour. The aromas of this dish with cardamom and fenugreek seeds take the flavours to the next level, making it a mouth-watering, addicting soup.

Roasted Corn Chowder with Cardamom and Fenugreek

4 Tbsp (60 mL) grapeseed oil

6 corn on the cob, husks removed

1 Tbsp (15 mL) Italian seasoning mix

1 tsp (5 mL) cardamom seeds

1 tsp (5 mL) fenugreek seeds

¼ tsp (1 mL) ground cloves

¼ tsp (1 mL) red chili flakes

salt and pepper to taste

1 medium onion, chopped

3 medium potatoes, boiled and mashed

2 cups (500 mL) vegetable broth

¼ cup (60 mL) sour cream

fresh basil or cilantro for garnish

Preheat the grill to medium. Using 2 Tbsp (30 mL) of the oil, rub each cob of corn generously with oil. Gently place the cobs on the grill and cook until all sides are golden brown, about 8 to 10 minutes. Let them cool, then remove the kernels using a serrated knife. Set aside.

In a large saucepan on medium-high, heat the remaining 2 Tbsp (30 mL) oil and cook the Italian seasoning, cardamom seeds, fenugreek seeds, cloves, chili flakes, salt and pepper for 30 seconds. Add the onion and cook, stirring frequently, until the onion is tender, about 3 minutes. Add the potatoes, broth and sour cream and whisk until well mixed. Reduce the heat to low and simmer for 2 to 4 minutes. Add the corn kernels to the broth. Cook for another 2 minutes.

To serve, garnish each bowl with fresh basil. **SERVES 4**

This recipe is inspired by raita, a yogurt dish served with spicy curries to soothe their heat in your mouth. I often make raita even when I don't have hot curry. I decided to add this recipe to my soup collection because I really like it, and hope you enjoy it as well.

Cold Yogurt Soup with Fennel, Basil and Pine Nuts

Whisk all the ingredients together in a large bowl until fully blended.

Serve in shallow bowls with your favourite crackers. Enjoy! **SERVES 4 TO 6**

3 cups (750 mL) plain yogurt

1 cup (250 mL) 2% milk

¼ cup (60 mL) loosely packed chopped basil

1 Tbsp (15 mL) fennel seeds

1 Tbsp (15 mL) grated ginger

½ tsp (2 mL) smoked paprika

¼ tsp (1 mL) ground cardamom

2 Tbsp (30 mL) pine nuts, toasted

salt and pepper to taste

You will be surprised by how amazing this soup tastes. Garlic, ginger, mustard seeds and curry leaves make it irresistible by adding great flavours and textures. This dish makes a very nutritious vegetarian meal.

Mixed Lentils with Leek Soup

2 Tbsp (30 mL) grapeseed oil

1 Tbsp (15 mL) finely chopped garlic

1 Tbsp (15 mL) finely chopped ginger

15 curry leaves

1 Tbsp (15 mL) brown mustard seeds

1 Tbsp (15 mL) garam masala (see page 11)

1 tsp (5 mL) ground turmeric

salt and pepper to taste

1 cup (250 mL) mixed lentils

4 cups (1 L) vegetable broth

2 leeks, cleaned and finely chopped

In a large pot, heat the oil and cook the garlic and ginger for 2 minutes on medium-high, stirring frequently. Add the curry leaves, mustard seeds, garam masala, turmeric, salt and pepper, and cook for 30 seconds.

Add the lentils then the broth, 3 cups (750 mL) water and the leeks and bring to a boil. Turn down the heat to low and let the soup simmer, uncovered, until the lentils are fully cooked, 30 to 40 minutes. **SERVES 4 TO 6**

This recipe brings my favourite flavours together. The licorice from the fennel with the nuttiness from the black beans is a killer combination. What I enjoy here is the way the fennel seeds combine with the pungent flavours of mustard seeds and curry leaves.

Fennel and Black Bean Soup

3 Tbsp (45 mL) grapeseed oil

1 large fennel bulb, chopped

1 onion, chopped

1 Tbsp (15 mL) chopped garlic

2 large potatoes, peeled and cubed

4 cups (1 L) vegetable broth

1 Tbsp (15 mL) fennel seeds

1 tsp (5 mL) brown mustard seeds

¼ cup (60 mL) loosely packed fresh curry leaves

salt and pepper to taste

14 oz can (398 mL) black beans, drained and rinsed

In a large pot, heat 2 Tbsp (30 mL) of the oil and cook the fennel bulb, onion and garlic on medium-high for 3 to 4 minutes, stirring frequently, until the fennel and onion are tender.

Add the potatoes then the broth and bring to a boil. Reduce heat to medium-low and cook, covered, until the potatoes are fully cooked. Turn the heat off and let the mixture cool.

Purée in a food processor until all the vegetables are thoroughly blended.

In a skillet, heat the remaining 1 Tbsp (15 mL) oil and cook the fennel seeds, mustard seeds, curry leaves, salt and pepper on medium-high until the mustard seeds start popping, about 20 seconds. Add the black beans and cook for another 2 minutes, stirring frequently, until the beans are heated through.

Add the bean mixture to the fennel purée and stir thoroughly. Reheat before serving. **SERVES 4 TO 6**

Mussels and Curry Leaf Soup

2 Tbsp (30 mL) grapeseed oil

1 tsp (5 mL) asafoetida

¼ cup (60 mL) loosely packed fresh curry leaves

¼ cup (60 mL) fenugreek leaves

1 Tbsp (15 mL) crushed garlic

1 tsp (5 mL) ground turmeric

1 tsp (5 mL) smoked paprika

salt and pepper to taste

1 cup (250 mL) plain yogurt

1 Tbsp (15 mL) chickpea flour

1 can (330 mL) Indian lager

1 cup (250 mL) vegetable broth

3 lb (1.5 kg) mussels, rinsed and debearded

cilantro leaves for garnish

In a large saucepan, heat the oil on medium-high. Add the asafoetida and let it sizzle for 15 seconds. Add the curry leaves, fenugreek leaves, garlic, turmeric, paprika, salt and pepper and cook for 30 seconds.

In a large bowl, whisk together 4 cups (1 L) water, the yogurt and the chickpea flour. Add the yogurt mixture to the saucepan. Bring the mixture to a boil, then reduce the heat to low and simmer, uncovered, until thickened, 20 to 30 minutes.

While the soup is simmering, in a separate large pot, bring the lager and vegetable broth to a boil. Add the mussels and cover the pot with a lid. Cook until the mussels are open, about 10 minutes. Discard any unopened ones. Strain the opened mussels and let them cool, then remove them from their shells.

To serve, divide the soup among 4 serving bowls. Place the mussels in the middle of each bowl and sprinkle with cilantro. **SERVES 4**

I always buy both dried and fresh sage. I use the dried herb for cleansing ceremonies in my house, and use fresh sage for soups. I love the aroma and taste of sage and frequently combine it with rosemary. But for this recipe I decided to add the citrusy flavour of coriander and pungent flavours of mustard seeds and curry leaves to create this brightly flavoured soup.

Shredded Chicken and Sage Soup

2 Tbsp (30 mL) grapeseed oil

1 medium onion, chopped

1 Tbsp (15 mL) ground coriander

1 tsp (5 mL) brown mustard seeds

salt and pepper to taste

2 boneless, skinless chicken breasts, cubed

6 cups (1.5 L) vegetable broth

1 cup (250 mL) frozen peas

3 Tbsp (45 mL) chopped fresh sage

In a large pot, heat the oil and cook the onion on medium-high for 2 minutes, stirring frequently. Add the coriander, mustard seeds, salt and pepper and cook for 30 seconds. Add the rest of the ingredients and bring to a boil. Reduce the heat to low and let the soup simmer, covered, for 20 to 25 minutes before serving. **SERVES 4 TO 6**

With beef, vegetables and fresh herbs, this soup is the best way to fight off any cold or flu during winter. The flavours are addicting, and the soup is very easy to make, especially if you use frozen vegetables.

Beefy Vegetable Soup with Fresh Herbs

3 Tbsp (45 mL) grapeseed oil

1 lb (500 g) beef, cut in small cubes

1 Tbsp (15 mL) garam masala (see page 11)

1 tsp (5 mL) ground turmeric

4 bay leaves

6 cups (1.5 L) vegetable broth

4 cups (1 L) mixed vegetables, chopped in ½-inch (1 cm) pieces

1 cup (250 mL) frozen corn

1 tsp (5 mL) chopped fresh thyme

1 Tbsp (15 mL) chopped fresh oregano

1 Tbsp (15 mL) chopped fresh basil

salt and pepper to taste

In a skillet, heat 1 Tbsp (15 mL) of the oil on medium heat. Add the cubed beef and cook until the juices turn brown, 3 to 5 minutes. Set aside.

In a large pot, combine the remaining oil and the rest of the ingredients, except the beef, and bring the soup to a boil. Turn down the heat and let it simmer, covered, until the vegetables are fully cooked, about 15 minutes. Add the beef and cook for 2 minutes to heat through before serving. **SERVES 4 TO 6**

salads

Daikon and Cherry Tomatoes with Cumin Dressing / 38

Red Pepper, Turnip and Cilantro with Grapefruit Dressing / 39

Turnip Salad with Warm Mustard Dressing / 40

Goodness of Beans and Toasted Coconut / 41

Grilled Romaine Lettuce and Mango with Raspberry Dressing / 42

Dijon Fruit Salad / 44

Grilled Corn and Baby Cucumber with Lemon Mint Dressing / 45

Poached Pears and Grilled Tomatoes with Cranberry Arugula / 46

Steamed Chard with Candied Pecans and Mango Dressing / 48

Baked Kale and Bocconcini with Sugarcane Pomegranate Dressing / 50

Fried Paneer with Wild Greens and Hummus Dressing / 51

Baked Beets with Bocconcini and Fresh Ginger Dressing / 52

Beets and Fried Goat Cheese with Fenugreek Dressing / 53

Crispy Scallops with Grilled Beans and Cherry Tomato Dressing / 54

Lobster and Grilled Asparagus with Coriander Dressing / 55

Lobster with Prawns and Paprika Coriander Dressing / 57

Daikon has a strong, sharp taste, and mixed with the cherry tomatoes and spiced dressing it combines all the flavours my palate requires. The thinner, smaller daikons have a much sharper flavour than the large thick ones, which add more sweetness. Follow your palate to choose your desired daikon in this salad.

Daikon and Cherry Tomatoes with Cumin Dressing

2 medium daikons

2 cups (500 mL) cherry tomatoes

Cumin Dressing

¼ cup (60 mL) olive oil

1 Tbsp (15 mL) finely chopped ginger

1 tsp (5 mL) cumin seeds

1 tsp (5 mL) ground cumin

tsp (2 mL) smoked paprika

1 Tbsp (15 mL) lemon juice

1 tsp (5 mL) lemon zest

salt and pepper to taste

Peel and thinly slice the daikon and halve the cherry tomatoes. Set aside.

TO MAKE THE DRESSING In a skillet, heat the oil and cook the ginger on medium-high until the ginger is cooked, about 30 seconds. Add the ground cumin and seeds, paprika, lemon juice and zest, salt and pepper and cook for 20 seconds. Turn off the heat and let it cool.

TO PLATE THE DISH Arrange the daikon slices on a salad plate, then top with cherry tomatoes and drizzle with Cumin Dressing. **SERVES 4**

This is a simple salad. I often make it when I am cooking a heavy meal and need something light as a starter. I created the grapefruit dressing because grapefruit has a very clear, tangy flavour and complements my spices nicely.

Red Pepper, Turnip and Cilantro with Grapefruit Dressing

2 red bell peppers, seeds removed and thinly sliced

1 medium turnip, peeled and thinly sliced

1 small bunch of cilantro, leaves removed from the stem

Grapefruit Dressing

¼ cup (60 mL) flaxseed oil

½ cup (125 mL) grapefruit juice

zest of 1 small grapefruit

¼ tsp (1 mL) ground coriander

salt and pepper to taste

Toss the red peppers, turnip and cilantro in a bowl.

TO PREPARE THE DRESSING Thoroughly whisk the oil, grapefruit juice and zest, coriander, salt and pepper in a deep bowl.

TO PLATE THE DISH Place a small mound of pepper-turnip salad on the plate and drizzle with Grapefruit Dressing. **SERVES 4**

The sharp flavours of turnip and radish and the freshness of cucumbers make this salad a refreshing gift for your taste buds. The warm earthy flavours of the spices in the dressing add the perfect touch to the dish.

Turnip Salad with Warm Mustard Dressing

1 large turnip

1 large English cucumber

½ lb (250 g) radishes

1 small red onion

Warm Mustard Dressing

¼ cup (60 mL) flaxseed oil

2 Tbsp (30 mL) dried oregano leaves

1 Tbsp (15 mL) brown mustard seeds

1 tsp (5 mL) ground cumin

1 tsp (5 mL) crushed garlic

½ tsp (2 mL) cardamom seeds, partially crushed

Peel and thinly slice the turnip. Thinly slice the cucumber, radishes and onion and set aside.

TO PREPARE THE DRESSING In a small skillet, heat the oil for 10 seconds on medium-high. Add the oregano, mustard seeds, cumin, garlic and cardamom seeds and cook on medium-high for 30 seconds.

TO PLATE THE DISH Place a layer of turnip slices on a large plate, then arrange the cucumber, radish and onion slices on top. Drizzle the Warm Mustard Dressing over all. **SERVES 4**

I teach in an elementary school, and I find myself playing with the kids in the playground during lunch, so I want to make sure I have a quick and healthy lunch to eat. This is a perfect lunch to take for your breaks. The longer the beans sit in the dressing, the more flavourful this salad becomes. I always mix in the coconut chips at the last minute because I like their crunchy nuttiness.

Goodness of Beans and Toasted Coconut

14 oz (398 mL) can mixed beans, drained and rinsed

2 green onions, both white and green parts finely chopped

¼ cup (60 mL) flat-leaf parsley, finely chopped

1 jalapeño chili, finely chopped

2 Tbsp (30 mL) red wine vinegar

1 Tbsp (15 mL) lime juice

¼ tsp (1 mL) ground cumin

¼ tsp (1 mL) ground cardamom

¼ cup (60 mL) dried coconut slices, slightly toasted (see sidebar)

Toss everything except the coconut slices into a large bowl.

Sprinkle with coconut chips before serving. Serve chilled. **SERVES 4**

HOW TO TOAST COCONUT SLICES

Heat a skillet on low heat. Toast the coconut slices, stirring frequently, until they turn golden brown, about 30 seconds to 1 minute.

How could you ever go wrong with grilled mango and romaine? You just can't, especially when it is combined with the warm earthy flavour of ground cumin. I also use cumin seeds here because I like the strong flavour and crunchy texture. I toast them lightly for just 15 to 20 seconds on medium-low heat.

Grilled Romaine Lettuce and Mango with Raspberry Dressing

2 Tbsp (30 mL) honey

1 Tbsp (15 mL) lemon juice

2 large ripe mangoes, peeled and sliced

2 heads romaine lettuce

¼ tsp (1 mL) ground cardamom

¼ tsp (1 mL) ground cloves

¼ tsp (1 mL) smoked paprika

Raspberry Dressing

½ cup (125 mL) raspberries

¼ cup (60 mL) flaxseed oil

1 Tbsp (15 mL) lemon juice

1 tsp (5 mL) Dijon mustard

¼ tsp (1 mL) ground cumin

¼ tsp (1 mL) cumin seeds, toasted

salt and pepper to taste

Heat the grill to medium-high. Combine the honey and lemon juice in a bowl. Brush the honey mixture on the mango slices and romaine leaves. Grill the mango and lettuce until they are lightly charred, about 3 to 5 minutes. Remove from the grill and sprinkle with cardamom, cloves and paprika.

TO PREPARE THE DRESSING In a blender, mix the raspberries, oil, lemon juice, mustard, ground cumin, cumin seeds, salt and pepper until the raspberries are mixed well in the oil.

TO PLATE THE DISH Arrange romaine and mango slices on a plate and drizzle with Raspberry Dressing.

SERVES 4

GRILLED ROMAINE LETTUCE AND MANGO WITH
RASPBERRY DRESSING (LEFT), RASPBERRY DRESSING
(TOP RIGHT), BAKED KALE AND BOCCONCINI WITH
SUGARCANE POMEGRANATE DRESSING (PAGE 50)
(BOTTOM RIGHT)

You can serve this as a dessert or a salad. The rich spice flavours are infused into the pears as they poach. I use grilled tomato here, but you can use grilled red pepper or even zucchini to add a different flavour. In the dressing, try chopped red grapes instead of cranberries.

Poached Pears and Grilled Tomatoes with Cranberry Arugula

Poached Pears

1 cup (250 mL) sugar

14 whole cloves

12 green cardamom pods

6 whole star anise

2 Tbsp (30 mL) fresh lemon juice

zest of 1 lemon

2 pears, peeled, seeded and thickly sliced

Grilled Tomatoes

1 Tbsp (15 mL) grapeseed oil

1 Tbsp (15 mL) garam masala (see page 11)

salt and pepper to taste

4 medium tomatoes, sliced into thick rounds

Cranberry Arugula

⅓ cup (80 mL) olive oil

¼ cup (60 mL) dried cranberries

juice and zest of 1 lemon

1 tsp (5 mL) smoked paprika

salt and pepper to taste

few handfuls of arugula

FOR THE PEARS In a saucepan, combine all the ingredients except the pears with 4 cups (1 L) water. Bring to a boil, turn down the heat and let simmer for 5 minutes. Add the pears and cook for 12 to 15 minutes, until they can be easily pierced by a fork. Set aside.

FOR THE TOMATOES While the pears are cooking, prepare the grilled tomatoes. Heat the grill to medium-high. In a bowl, mix together the oil, garam masala, salt and pepper and brush the mixture on both sides of the tomato slices. Gently place the tomatoes on the grill and cook on both sides until they are partially charred, about 3 to 5 minutes.

FOR THE DRESSING With a hand blender, thoroughly purée the olive oil, cranberries, lemon juice and zest, paprika, salt and pepper. In a large bowl, gently toss the arugula with the dressing.

TO PLATE THE DISH Place a small handful of the Cranberry Arugula on each plate and top with a few pear slices and a few tomato slices. **SERVES 4 TO 6**

SUGGESTED WINE
2011 Freudian Sip by Therapy Vineyards

GRILLED ROMAINE LETTUCE AND MANGO WITH
RASPBERRY DRESSING (LEFT), RASPBERRY DRESSING
(TOP RIGHT), BAKED KALE AND BOCCONCINI WITH
SUGARCANE POMEGRANATE DRESSING (PAGE 50)
(BOTTOM RIGHT)

You can serve this as a dessert or a salad. The rich spice flavours are infused into the pears as they poach. I use grilled tomato here, but you can use grilled red pepper or even zucchini to add a different flavour. In the dressing, try chopped red grapes instead of cranberries.

Poached Pears and Grilled Tomatoes with Cranberry Arugula

Poached Pears

1 cup (250 mL) sugar

14 whole cloves

12 green cardamom pods

6 whole star anise

2 Tbsp (30 mL) fresh lemon juice

zest of 1 lemon

2 pears, peeled, seeded and thickly sliced

Grilled Tomatoes

1 Tbsp (15 mL) grapeseed oil

1 Tbsp (15 mL) garam masala (see page 11)

salt and pepper to taste

4 medium tomatoes, sliced into thick rounds

Cranberry Arugula

⅓ cup (80 mL) olive oil

¼ cup (60 mL) dried cranberries

juice and zest of 1 lemon

1 tsp (5 mL) smoked paprika

salt and pepper to taste

few handfuls of arugula

FOR THE PEARS In a saucepan, combine all the ingredients except the pears with 4 cups (1 L) water. Bring to a boil, turn down the heat and let simmer for 5 minutes. Add the pears and cook for 12 to 15 minutes, until they can be easily pierced by a fork. Set aside.

FOR THE TOMATOES While the pears are cooking, prepare the grilled tomatoes. Heat the grill to medium-high. In a bowl, mix together the oil, garam masala, salt and pepper and brush the mixture on both sides of the tomato slices. Gently place the tomatoes on the grill and cook on both sides until they are partially charred, about 3 to 5 minutes.

FOR THE DRESSING With a hand blender, thoroughly purée the olive oil, cranberries, lemon juice and zest, paprika, salt and pepper. In a large bowl, gently toss the arugula with the dressing.

TO PLATE THE DISH Place a small handful of the Cranberry Arugula on each plate and top with a few pear slices and a few tomato slices. **SERVES 4 TO 6**

SUGGESTED WINE
2011 Freudian Sip by Therapy Vineyards

GRILLED ROMAINE LETTUCE AND MANGO WITH RASPBERRY DRESSING (LEFT), RASPBERRY DRESSING (TOP RIGHT), BAKED KALE AND BOCCONCINI WITH SUGARCANE POMEGRANATE DRESSING (PAGE 50) (BOTTOM RIGHT)

You can serve this as a dessert or a salad. The rich spice flavours are infused into the pears as they poach. I use grilled tomato here, but you can use grilled red pepper or even zucchini to add a different flavour. In the dressing, try chopped red grapes instead of cranberries.

Poached Pears and Grilled Tomatoes with Cranberry Arugula

Poached Pears

1 cup (250 mL) sugar

14 whole cloves

12 green cardamom pods

6 whole star anise

2 Tbsp (30 mL) fresh lemon juice

zest of 1 lemon

2 pears, peeled, seeded and thickly sliced

Grilled Tomatoes

1 Tbsp (15 mL) grapeseed oil

1 Tbsp (15 mL) garam masala (see page 11)

salt and pepper to taste

4 medium tomatoes, sliced into thick rounds

Cranberry Arugula

⅓ cup (80 mL) olive oil

¼ cup (60 mL) dried cranberries

juice and zest of 1 lemon

1 tsp (5 mL) smoked paprika

salt and pepper to taste

few handfuls of arugula

FOR THE PEARS In a saucepan, combine all the ingredients except the pears with 4 cups (1 L) water. Bring to a boil, turn down the heat and let simmer for 5 minutes. Add the pears and cook for 12 to 15 minutes, until they can be easily pierced by a fork. Set aside.

FOR THE TOMATOES While the pears are cooking, prepare the grilled tomatoes. Heat the grill to medium-high. In a bowl, mix together the oil, garam masala, salt and pepper and brush the mixture on both sides of the tomato slices. Gently place the tomatoes on the grill and cook on both sides until they are partially charred, about 3 to 5 minutes.

FOR THE DRESSING With a hand blender, thoroughly purée the olive oil, cranberries, lemon juice and zest, paprika, salt and pepper. In a large bowl, gently toss the arugula with the dressing.

TO PLATE THE DISH Place a small handful of the Cranberry Arugula on each plate and top with a few pear slices and a few tomato slices. **SERVES 4 TO 6**

SUGGESTED WINE
2011 Freudian Sip by Therapy Vineyards

Chard has high amounts of fibre and protein and a great taste. I like its pungent flavour, which pairs very nicely with spices such as garam masala. The sweet flavours from the candied pecans and rich juicy flavours from the mango make this salad so appealing.

Steamed Chard with Candied Pecans and Mango Dressing

Mango Dressing

¼ cup (60 mL) flaxseed oil

¼ cup (60 mL) finely chopped mango

¼ cup (60 mL) mango juice

3 Tbsp (45 mL) lemon juice

½ tsp (2 mL) crushed garlic

½ tsp (2 mL) smoked paprika

½ tsp (2 mL) garam masala (see page 11)

salt and pepper to taste

Candied Pecans

1 egg white

1 Tbsp (15 mL) water

1 cup (250 mL) sugar

½ tsp (2 mL) ground fennel

¼ tsp (1 mL) ground cloves

¼ tsp (1 mL) ground cardamom

¼ tsp (1 mL) salt

2 cups (500 mL) pecan halves

TO PREPARE THE DRESSING In a bowl, thoroughly whisk the oil, mango and mango juice, lemon juice, garlic, paprika, garam masala, salt and pepper. Set aside.

TO PREPARE THE PECANS Preheat the oven to 300°F (150°C). In a bowl, whisk the egg white with the water until it turns frothy. In a different bowl, mix together the sugar, fennel, cloves, cardamom and salt. Coat the pecans in the egg mixture, then add them to the spice mixture and stir until well coated. Place them on a greased pan and bake for 30 to 40 minutes, turning them every 15 minutes. Remove from the oven and let cool.

Steamed Chard

1 bunch chard

2 Tbsp (30 mL) grapeseed oil

¼ tsp (1 mL) smoked paprika

¼ tsp (1 mL) ground fennel

2 Tbsp (30 mL) lemon juice

1 cup (250 mL) feta cheese

TO PREPARE THE CHARD While the pecans are cooling, prepare the chard. Wash the leaves and remove the stems. Slice the stems into shorter lengths and sauté in the oil in a skillet on medium-high until cooked, about 3 to 4 minutes. Set aside.

Steam the chard leaves in a steamer until wilted, about 4 to 6 minutes. Remove them from the steamer and mix with the paprika, fennel, lemon juice and the cooked stems.

TO PLATE THE DISH Arrange the chard on a plate, top with crumbled feta and then the candied pecans. Drizzle Mango Dressing overtop. **SERVES 4**

I can't get enough of baked kale—it's healthy and very flavourful. In this recipe, it adds a wonderful crunchy texture to the tomatoes and bocconcini. Finishing this dish with the pomegranate dressing creates real magic on the plate.

Baked Kale and Bocconcini with Sugarcane Pomegranate Dressing

Sugarcane Pomegranate Dressing

2 Tbsp (30 mL) oil

½ tsp (2 mL) crushed garlic

¼ cup (60 mL) pomegranate seeds

½-inch (1 cm) piece sugarcane

½ tsp (2 mL) ground coriander

¼ tsp (1 mL) smoked paprika

salt and pepper to taste

Baked Kale

6–7 kale leaves

1 Tbsp (15 mL) grapeseed oil

1 tsp (5 mL) garam masala (see page 11)

2 medium tomatoes, sliced

2 large bocconcini, thinly sliced

2 Tbsp (30 mL) freshly shaved Parmesan cheese

TO MAKE THE DRESSING Heat the oil and cook the garlic in a skillet on medium-high, stirring frequently, until the garlic is cooked, about 1 minute. Add the pomegranate seeds, sugarcane, coriander, paprika, salt and pepper and cook for 20 seconds. Make sure the sugarcane is mixed in well. Remove from the heat.

TO PREPARE THE KALE Preheat the oven to 350°F (175°C). Tear the kale leaves into bite-size pieces and remove the thick stem. Place the pieces on a baking sheet and sprinkle with the oil and garam masala. Bake until the leaves turn crisp, about 8 to 10 minutes. Remove from the oven.

TO PLATE THE DISH Arrange the tomato slices on a plate and top with bocconcini slices and warm kale chips. Sprinkle with Parmesan cheese, then drizzle with Sugarcane Pomegranate Dressing. **SERVES 4**

Pictured on page 43.

I use whole milk for the paneer in this recipe because it is a little creamier, but if you want to make paneer often and are worried about fat content, use 2% milk. It will still have enough cream content and it is healthy as well. The Hummus Dressing was my daughter, Anoop's, idea and I am proud of her for introducing it to this recipe, as it works very well.

Fried Paneer with Wild Greens and Hummus Dressing

2 cups (500 mL) paneer, cubed (see sidebar)

¼ cup (60 mL) grapeseed oil

Hummus Dressing

14 oz (398 mL) can chickpeas

½ cup (125 mL) loosely packed mint leaves

¼ cup (60 mL) olive oil

juice of 1 medium lemon

1 small green chili, finely chopped, seeds removed

2 Tbsp (30 mL) sesame seeds

1 Tbsp (15 mL) garlic, finely chopped

1 tsp (5 mL) garam masala (see page 11)

salt and pepper to taste

1 bag mixed greens (baby spinach, baby lettuce and arugula)

1 small red onion, thinly sliced

In a non-stick skillet on medium-high, fry the paneer in the oil, stirring frequently, until it is golden brown on all sides, about 3 to 5 minutes. Set aside.

FOR THE DRESSING Blend the chickpeas, mint, oil, lemon juice, chili, sesame seeds, garlic, garam masala, salt and pepper in a food processor until smooth.

TO PLATE THE DISH Place a handful of greens and a few onion slices on a salad plate. Add 2 Tbsp (30 mL) of Hummus Dressing and mix it in well. Sprinkle one-quarter of the paneer cubes overtop. Store the leftover dressing in the fridge for up to one week. **SERVES 4**

To Make Your Own Paneer

8 cups (2 L) whole milk   *¼ cup (60 mL) white vinegar*

In a saucepan, bring the milk to a boil, add the vinegar and turn off the heat. Strain the water from the curd by pouring the liquid through cheesecloth set into a colander over a bowl. Put a heavy weight on the curd to press out all the whey and let it sit for about 20 minutes.

Remove the paneer block from the cheesecloth and cut it into small blocks. Store in an airtight container in the fridge for up to one week. **MAKES 2 CUPS (500 ML)**

This recipe evolved when my son decided to throw a beet in the toaster oven and turn it on. He had seen me baking sweet potatoes and thought it would be great to do the same thing with beets.

Baked Beets with Bocconcini and Fresh Ginger Dressing

4 medium beets

Ginger Dressing

¼ cup (60 mL) flaxseed oil

juice of half a lemon

1 Tbsp (15 mL) finely chopped ginger

¼ tsp (1 mL) brown mustard seeds, toasted

salt and pepper to taste

2 large bocconcini, thinly sliced

4 tomatoes, thinly sliced

¼ cup (60 mL) cilantro leaves

Preheat the oven to 375°F (190°C). Bake the beets until cooked, about 45 minutes. Let them cool, then peel the skin off and thinly slice them.

TO MAKE THE DRESSING Thoroughly mix the oil, lemon juice, ginger, mustard seeds, salt and pepper in a bowl.

TO PLATE THE DISH Arrange a layer of beet slices and top them with bocconcini and tomato slices. Garnish with cilantro and drizzle with Ginger Dressing. **SERVES 4**

The colours of this salad are so beautiful that you would not want to eat it before taking a picture—at least, that happens in my kitchen with my 19-year-old daughter. Fenugreek dressing is something you will fall in love with and want to make often because it adds a unique touch to the entire dish. A spicy twist would be to sprinkle 1 Tbsp (15 mL) of garam masala (see page 11) overtop sliced beets, and bake them, covered in foil, for about 30 minutes.

Beets and Fried Goat Cheese with Fenugreek Dressing

2 large beets, peeled and thinly sliced

14 oz (400 g) goat cheese log

2 Tbsp (30 mL) garam masala (see page 11)

1 Tbsp (15 mL) smoked paprika

salt and pepper to taste

¼ cup (60 mL) grapeseed oil

Fenugreek Dressing

¼ cup (60 mL) grapeseed oil

¼ cup (60 mL) dried fenugreek leaves

1 Tbsp (15 mL) lemon juice

½ tsp (2 mL) lemon zest

1 Tbsp (15 mL) finely chopped ginger

¼ tsp (1 mL) ground cloves

salt and pepper to taste

In a saucepan, boil the beets in water until tender, about 8 to 10 minutes. Drain the beets and set aside.

Cut the goat cheese into ¼-inch (0.6 cm) slices with fishing line or dental floss. On a shallow plate, mix together the garam masala, paprika, salt and pepper. Dip each side of the goat cheese in the spice mixture.

In a non-stick skillet, heat the oil on medium-high. Gently place the goat cheese slices in the oil and cook for 10 seconds on each side. Remove and set aside.

FOR THE DRESSING In a skillet, heat the oil and cook the fenugreek leaves, lemon juice and zest, ginger, cloves, salt and pepper on medium-high for 30 seconds. Let cool.

TO PLATE THE DISH Place the beet slices on the plate and gently arrange the goat cheese on top. Drizzle with Fenugreek Dressing. **SERVES 4**

This salad is the perfect balance of great looks and amazing flavours, plus it's very easy to make.

Crispy Scallops with Grilled Beans and Cherry Tomato Dressing

Crispy Scallops

¼ cup (60 mL) dried fenugreek leaves

2 Tbsp (30 mL) garam masala (see page 11)

2 Tbsp (30 mL) smoked paprika

1 Tbsp (15 mL) ground coriander

1 tsp (5 mL) ground cardamom

1 tsp (5 mL) dried oregano

½ tsp (2 mL) garlic powder

salt and pepper to taste

20 medium scallops

¼ cup (60 mL) grapeseed oil

Grilled Beans

1 lb (500 g) green beans

1 Tbsp (15 mL) grapeseed oil

pinch of salt

Cherry Tomato Dressing

1 cup (250 mL) cherry tomatoes

3 Tbsp (45 mL) flaxseed oil

2 Tbsp (30 mL) white wine vinegar

1 Tbsp (15 mL) brown sugar

1 small green chili, chopped (keep the seeds if you like the heat)

salt and pepper to taste

Mix together the fenugreek leaves, garam masala, paprika, coriander, cardamom, oregano, garlic, salt and pepper and spread it out on a shallow plate.

In a non-stick pan, heat the oil on medium-high. Dip the scallops into the spice mixture and place them spiced side down in the oil. Cook until the spice mixture turns golden and crispy, about 1 to 2 minutes. Turn the scallops gently and cook until done, about 3 minutes. Set aside.

FOR THE GRILLED BEANS Preheat the grill to medium-high. Brush the beans with the oil and sprinkle with salt. Gently place the green beans on the grill and cook for 4 to 6 minutes, until the beans turn slightly brown but still have a little crunch. Don't overcook. Remove them from the grill and set aside.

FOR THE CHERRY TOMATO DRESSING Blend the tomatoes, oil, vinegar, sugar, chili, salt and pepper in a food processor until smooth.

TO PLATE THE DISH Spoon 2 Tbsp (30 mL) of Cherry Tomato Dressing on a plate. Gently set one-quarter of the beans on it. Place 5 scallops on top of the beans, spiced side up. SERVES 4

During the filming of Spice Goddess, *I spent many summers in Halifax—a town of fabulous juicy lobsters. After trying a lobster dish in a local restaurant, I knew in my heart that I had to incorporate it with my spices, and I was right. It worked beautifully. This is a simple and very elegant salad that will impress your friends and loved ones.*

Lobster and Grilled Asparagus with Coriander Dressing

4 lobster tails, steamed and meat removed (see sidebar)

Coriander Dressing

¼ cup (60 mL) flaxseed oil

¼ cup (60 mL) loosely packed finely chopped basil

½ tsp (2 mL) ground coriander

¼ tsp (1 mL) cardamom seeds

1 green chili, finely chopped (keep the seeds if you like the heat)

juice and zest of 1 lemon

Grilled Asparagus

1 lb (500 g) asparagus, hard ends removed

2 Tbsp (30 mL) grapeseed oil

TO PREPARE THE DRESSING Whisk together the oil, basil, coriander, cardamom seeds, chili, lemon juice and zest. Set aside.

TO PREPARE THE ASPARAGUS Preheat the grill to medium-high. Brush the oil on the asparagus and grill until they are cooked but still have some crunch, about 6 to 8 minutes.

TO PLATE THE DISH Mix the lobster with the asparagus and drizzle with Coriander Dressing. **SERVES 4**

HOW TO COOK LOBSTER TAILS
In a large saucepan, bring 8 to 10 cups (2 to 2.5 L) of water and a generous amount of salt to a boil. Add the lobster tails and cook for 10 to 12 minutes, until the lobster meat is completely white with no translucence. Let cool, then remove the meat from the shell.

My daughter, Anoop's, love for seafood inspired me to create this recipe. Once the lobster and prawns are cooked, the rest of the steps are very simple. You just throw everything together for a very elegant salad. If you like this half as much as Anoop does, you'll be eating it all the time!

Lobster with Prawns and Paprika Coriander Dressing

4 lobster tails, steamed and meat removed (see page 55)

20 cooked prawns (see sidebar)

1 medium purple onion, finely chopped

1 cup (250 mL) basil leaves, chopped

Paprika Coriander Dressing

¼ cup (60 mL) flaxseed oil

juice of 1 lemon

1 tsp (5 mL) smoked paprika

½ tsp (2 mL) ground coriander

salt and pepper to taste

Combine the lobster, prawns, onion and basil leaves in a salad bowl.

TO PREPARE THE DRESSING Thoroughly whisk the oil, lemon juice, paprika, coriander, salt and pepper in a bowl.

TO SERVE Drizzle the dressing over the salad. **SERVES 4**

||||||||||||||||||||||||||||||||||||||||||||
SUGGESTED WINE
2010 White Lie by Serendipity Winery

||||||||||||||||||||||||||||||||||||||||||||||||||||||
HOW TO COOK PRAWNS
In a skillet, heat 2 Tbsp (30 mL) grapeseed oil on medium heat. Add 20 prawns, deveined and shells removed, and cook until they curl up and are just firm, about 3 to 5 minutes.

vegetables

GRILLED ROMAINE LETTUCE AND MANGO WITH
RASPBERRY DRESSING (LEFT), RASPBERRY DRESSING
(TOP RIGHT), BAKED KALE AND BOCCONCINI WITH
SUGARCANE POMEGRANATE DRESSING (PAGE 50)
(BOTTOM RIGHT)

When my daughter, Anoop, and her friends eat this salad, they tell me I should serve it as a dessert because it tastes so delicious. When teenagers like a recipe, I know for sure it is going to be a hit in my cookbook. Enjoy!

Dijon Fruit Salad

1 whole pineapple, peeled and cut into rings

1 mango, peeled, pitted and cut into thick slices

1 Tbsp (15 mL) grapeseed oil

¼ cup (60 mL) flaxseed oil or extra-virgin olive oil

1 Tbsp (15 mL) honey

1 Tbsp (15 mL) lemon juice

1 tsp (5 mL) Dijon mustard

½ tsp (2 mL) ground coriander

salt and pepper to taste

4 fresh figs, quartered

1 cup (250 mL) cherry tomatoes, halved

¼ cup (60 mL) minced red onion

2 Tbsp (30 mL) minced fresh mint

Brush the pineapple and mango with the grapeseed oil and grill both sides until golden brown, about 3 to 5 minutes per side. When cool, cut into bite-size pieces. Set aside.

Whisk the flaxseed oil, honey, lemon juice, mustard, coriander and salt and pepper in the bottom of a salad bowl. Add the pineapple and mango pieces and the figs, tomatoes, onion and mint and toss well. Let sit for 5 minutes before serving. **SERVES 4 TO 6**

When fresh corn arrives at the farmers market, I buy lots and use it to create many recipes. For this salad, I remove the husk and grill the corn, then remove the kernels. Sometimes I add grapes, tomatoes or even mangoes along with a sprinkle of ground cardamom and fennel. This is my all-time favourite patio salad.

Grilled Corn and Baby Cucumber with Lemon Mint Dressing

4 cobs of corn, husks removed

Lemon Mint Dressing

¼ cup (60 mL) flaxseed oil

¼ cup (60 mL) loosely packed chopped mint leaves

1 tsp (5 mL) toasted cumin seeds

¼ tsp (1 mL) red chili flakes

salt and pepper to taste

juice of 1 lemon

1 cup (250 mL) baby cucumbers, diced

¼ cup (60 mL) toasted pine nuts

Barbecue the corn over medium heat until it is golden brown and cooked through, about 8 to 10 minutes. Let the cobs cool and remove the kernels with a serrated knife.

TO MAKE THE DRESSING Combine the oil, mint leaves, cumin seeds, chili flakes, salt and pepper with the lemon juice in a bowl and whisk well.

TO PLATE THE DISH On each plate, place ¼ cup (60 mL) diced cucumber, one-quarter of the corn kernels and 1 Tbsp (15 mL) pine nuts. Drizzle with Lemon Mint Dressing. **SERVES 4**

You can serve this as a dessert or a salad. The rich spice flavours are infused into the pears as they poach. I use grilled tomato here, but you can use grilled red pepper or even zucchini to add a different flavour. In the dressing, try chopped red grapes instead of cranberries.

Poached Pears and Grilled Tomatoes with Cranberry Arugula

Poached Pears

1 cup (250 mL) sugar

14 whole cloves

12 green cardamom pods

6 whole star anise

2 Tbsp (30 mL) fresh lemon juice

zest of 1 lemon

2 pears, peeled, seeded and thickly sliced

Grilled Tomatoes

1 Tbsp (15 mL) grapeseed oil

1 Tbsp (15 mL) garam masala (see page 11)

salt and pepper to taste

4 medium tomatoes, sliced into thick rounds

Cranberry Arugula

⅓ cup (80 mL) olive oil

¼ cup (60 mL) dried cranberries

juice and zest of 1 lemon

1 tsp (5 mL) smoked paprika

salt and pepper to taste

few handfuls of arugula

FOR THE PEARS In a saucepan, combine all the ingredients except the pears with 4 cups (1 L) water. Bring to a boil, turn down the heat and let simmer for 5 minutes. Add the pears and cook for 12 to 15 minutes, until they can be easily pierced by a fork. Set aside.

FOR THE TOMATOES While the pears are cooking, prepare the grilled tomatoes. Heat the grill to medium-high. In a bowl, mix together the oil, garam masala, salt and pepper and brush the mixture on both sides of the tomato slices. Gently place the tomatoes on the grill and cook on both sides until they are partially charred, about 3 to 5 minutes.

FOR THE DRESSING With a hand blender, thoroughly purée the olive oil, cranberries, lemon juice and zest, paprika, salt and pepper. In a large bowl, gently toss the arugula with the dressing.

TO PLATE THE DISH Place a small handful of the Cranberry Arugula on each plate and top with a few pear slices and a few tomato slices. **SERVES 4 TO 6**

SUGGESTED WINE
2011 Freudian Sip by Therapy Vineyards

I've served pan-fried zucchini as an appetizer. Then I found myself making this sauce for the leftovers, to eat with rice for dinner. I decided to add this recipe for you because it has become one of the regular dishes I make for family guests.

Pan-fried Zucchini with Cilantro Coconut Sauce

Pan-fried Zucchini

2 Tbsp (30 mL) grapeseed oil

1 tsp (5 mL) ground cumin

1 medium zucchini, thinly sliced

Cilantro Coconut Sauce

2 Tbsp (30 mL) grapeseed oil

1 Tbsp (15 mL) mild curry masala (see page 12)

1 Tbsp (15 mL) ginger, finely chopped

1 tsp (5 mL) ground coriander

1 tsp (5 mL) ground cumin

1 tsp (5 mL) fennel seeds

½ tsp (2 mL) ground cardamom

2 cups (500 mL) fresh cilantro leaves, washed and roughly chopped

14 oz (398 mL) can coconut milk

1 small green chili, minced (keep the seeds if you like the heat)

FOR THE ZUCCHINI In a non-stick skillet, heat the oil on medium-low. Sprinkle the ground cumin over the zucchini slices and pan-fry them until they are golden brown on both sides, about 4 minutes per side. Set aside.

FOR THE SAUCE Heat a skillet on medium-low and heat the oil. Cook the mild curry masala, ginger, coriander, cumin, fennel and cardamom for 1 minute, until the ginger is softened. Add the cilantro, coconut milk and green chili and cook until the coconut milk is heated and all the spices are infused, about 1 minute. Turn off the heat. Let the mixture cool. Pulse in a blender until smooth and well blended.

TO PLATE THE DISH Spoon some of the Cilantro Coconut Sauce into a shallow bowl. Gently place zucchini slices on top. Serve with rice and grilled vegetables. **SERVES 4**

Pictured on page 113.

I started giving my son, Aaron, broccoli when he was a baby, and now he thinks a meal is not complete if it's not included. He prefers it crunchy, so I barely cook it, maybe only two minutes, just enough to ensure all the spices are infused into the dish.

Garlic and Coriander Broccoli

2 Tbsp (30 mL) grapeseed oil

2 Tbsp (30 mL) garlic

1 Tbsp (15 mL) coriander seeds, partly crushed

¼ cup (60 mL) loosely packed fresh curry leaves

¼ tsp (1 mL) red chili flakes

salt and pepper to taste

2 broccoli heads, cut into small pieces

In a skillet, heat the oil and cook the garlic on medium-high until it turns golden brown, about 30 seconds. Add the coriander seeds, curry leaves, chili flakes, salt and pepper and cook for 10 seconds.

Add the broccoli and ¼ cup (60 mL) water. Stir to combine the ingredients, cover and cook until the broccoli is tender-crisp, about 3 to 5 minutes.

Serve with rice or quinoa. **SERVES 4**

In my kitchen, grated cauliflower is often used to fill rotis. When I have leftover grated cauliflower, I like to cook it with potatoes or peas. This recipe was served as a main dish in the village and eaten with rotis.

Grated Cauliflower with Peas

2 Tbsp (30 mL) grapeseed oil

1 onion, chopped

1 Tbsp (15 mL) grated ginger

1 Tbsp (15 mL) coriander seeds

1 Tbsp (15 mL) cumin seeds

1 tsp (5 mL) ground turmeric

salt to taste

1 tomato, chopped

1 small cauliflower, grated

1 cup (250 mL) frozen peas

Heat the oil in a large, non-stick skillet on medium-high. Add the onion and ginger and cook for 4 minutes. Stir in the spices and salt and cook for 15 seconds, then add the tomato and cauliflower and cook until they are tender, about 12 to 15 minutes.

Add the peas and cook for a few minutes until the peas are cooked and coated with the spices.

Serve with rotis. **SERVES 4**

Bitter melon is a very acquired taste. Since I have been eating them all my life, I look forward to finding them at the specialty market. This melon does have a bitter flavour, but if you peel the skin, infuse it with lots of salt and let it sit on the counter for a few hours, the bitterness mellows. The remaining bitter flavour combines well with the spices and caramelized onions.

Bitter Melon with Caramelized Onions

4 bitter melons

¼ cup (60 mL) salt

2 Tbsp (30 mL) grapeseed oil

2 onions, chopped

2 Tbsp (30 mL) grated ginger

4 large tomatoes, chopped

¼ cup (60 mL) loosely packed dried curry leaves

1 Tbsp (15 mL) garam masala (see page 11)

1 tsp (5 mL) mustard seeds

1 tsp (5 mL) ground turmeric

Peel the melons, cut them in half lengthwise and scoop out the pulp and seeds. Rub the salt all over the halves and let them sit on the counter for a few hours to reduce the bitterness. Rinse off most of the salt and cut the melons into thin slices.

Heat the oil in a skillet on medium-high, add the onion and ginger and cook for 4 minutes, until the onion is soft and golden. Add the tomatoes, curry leaves and spices. Cook for 30 seconds, stirring occasionally.

Add the melon slices to the onion-tomato mixture and cook, stirring frequently, until the bitter melon is soft, about 15 minutes.

Serve with rotis. **SERVES 4**

Pictured on page 75.

My mother made any vegetable taste so good, with a variety of ways of cooking them. For this dish, she would make a cut lengthwise in the okra after removing the hard end, and then fill them with her favourite spices. Then she would pan-fry the okra and serve it with rice. This is her recipe.

My Mother's Okra with Sautéed Tomatoes

Okra

1 lb (500 g) okra, washed, hard ends removed

2 Tbsp (30 mL) ground coriander

1 tsp (5 mL) ground turmeric

1 tsp (5 mL) smoked paprika

1 tsp (5 mL) salt

2 Tbsp (30 mL) grapeseed oil

Sautéed Tomatoes

2 Tbsp (30 mL) grapeseed oil

1 tsp (5 mL) cumin seeds

two 19 oz (540 mL) cans chopped tomatoes (about 4 cups/1 L)

salt and pepper to taste

FOR THE OKRA Make an incision down the middle of each okra from one end to the other.

Thoroughly mix the spices and salt in a bowl. Place a pinch of spice mixture in each okra.

Heat the oil in a large skillet on medium heat. Gently place the okra in the skillet and cook, stirring frequently, until they are golden brown and soft, about 6 to 8 minutes. Set aside.

FOR THE SAUTÉED TOMATOES Heat the oil in a large skillet on medium heat. Add the cumin seeds and cook for 10 seconds. Add the tomatoes, salt and pepper and turn down the heat to low. Cook until the tomatoes are softened, about 8 to 10 minutes.

TO SERVE Reheat the okra if necessary. Serve the okra and tomatoes with rice or rotis. **SERVES 4**

SUGGESTED WINE
2012 Gewürztraminer by Hillside Estate Winery

My friends tell me they do not know what to do with okra when they see it in a specialty market. They call me to ask for tips. I have given them this recipe and have gotten great feedback from all of them. The paneer is optional. You don't have to add it to the dish, as okra on its own is very delicious, especially when cooked with the right spices. I have also substituted feta for paneer many times.

Spiced Okra with Paneer

Heat the oil in a large skillet on medium-high. Add the spices and salt and cook for 30 seconds. Turn the heat to low. Add the okra and onion and cook until the okra is completely cooked, about 12 to 15 minutes.

Add the paneer and cook for another 2 minutes. Serve with rice. **SERVES 4**

2 Tbsp (30 mL) grapeseed oil

1 Tbsp (15 mL) garam masala (see page 11)

1 tsp (5 mL) black cumin seeds

1 tsp (5 mL) fenugreek seeds

¾ tsp (4 mL) asafoetida

pinch of salt

1 lb (500 g), okra, hard ends removed

2 medium onions, chopped

1 cup (250 mL) cubed paneer (see page 51)

There are so many different ways to cook eggplant. I like the grilling technique that I mention in the recipe for Mixed Lentils with Eggplant (page 74); my second-favourite way is this one. Traditionally, eggplants are cooked with potatoes, but since I have a sweet tooth it made sense to me to add yam to the eggplant. This is my regular choice for weekend lunches.

Cubed Eggplant with Yam

2 Tbsp (30 mL) grapeseed oil

1 red onion, chopped

2 Tbsp (30 mL) grated ginger

1 Tbsp (15 mL) garam masala (see page 11)

1 Tbsp (15 mL) fenugreek seeds

1 Tbsp (15 mL) cumin seeds

1 tsp (5 mL) ground turmeric

1 tsp (5 mL) red chili flakes

1 cup (250 mL) chopped tomatoes

1 large eggplant, cubed

1 medium yam, finely diced

salt and pepper to taste

Heat the oil in a large skillet on medium heat and add the onion and ginger. Cook until the onion is softened, about 4 minutes. Add the spices and toast for 10 seconds.

Add the tomatoes, eggplant, yam, salt and pepper and ¼ cup (60 mL) water and cook, stirring frequently, until the eggplant is tender, about 12 to 15 minutes.

Serve with rice or rotis. **SERVES 4**

My mother used to add fresh fenugreek leaves to corn rotis and served them with homemade yogurt. It takes a lot of practice to make corn rotis as it is very tricky to keep the roti in its shape. After several months of practice, I was able to master it. This recipe is much simpler but incorporates the wonderful flavours of pungent fenugreek leaves and nutty corn. A dollop of fresh yogurt before serving can be like icing on the cake.

Fresh Fenugreek Potatoes

1 Tbsp (15 mL) grapeseed oil

1 tsp (5 mL) grated garlic

2 tsp (10 mL) ground coriander

1 tsp (5 mL) brown mustard seeds

1 tsp (5 mL) ground cumin

2 tomatoes, chopped

pinch of salt and pepper

1 lb (500 g) fresh fenugreek, chopped

2 medium potatoes, thinly sliced

Heat the oil in a skillet on medium heat. Add the garlic and spices and cook for about 15 seconds. Add the tomatoes and season with salt and pepper, stirring well. Add the fenugreek and potatoes and about ½ cup (125 mL) water, and cook until the potatoes are tender, 8 to 10 minutes.

Serve with rotis. **SERVES 4**

Cauliflower is called gobi in Punjabi. When I was growing up, pakoras (vegetable fritters) were made for special occasions like weddings or festivals. Since they were a rare treat, I craved them all the time and looked forward to weddings in the village or festivals in town. This recipe is a tribute to all the great flavours I enjoyed growing up, and I know in my heart that you will love these flavours too.

Gobi Pakoras with Curry Sauce

Gobi Pakoras

1 cup (250 mL) finely grated cauliflower

¼ cup (60 mL) grated mozzarella cheese

2 Tbsp (30 mL) chickpea flour

2 Tbsp (30 mL) plain yogurt

1 Tbsp (15 mL) coriander seeds, partly crushed

1 tsp (5 mL) garam masala (see page 11)

salt and pepper to taste

3 Tbsp (45 mL) grapeseed oil

Curry Sauce

2 Tbsp (30 mL) grapeseed oil

1 Tbsp (15 mL) chopped garlic

1 Tbsp (15 mL) chopped ginger

1 Tbsp (15 mL) brown sugar

1 Tbsp (15 mL) garam masala (see page 11)

1 tsp (5 mL) smoked paprika

1 tsp (5 mL) ground coriander

½ tsp (2 mL) ground cardamom

salt and pepper to taste

14 oz (398 mL) can coconut milk

FOR THE PAKORAS In a medium bowl, thoroughly mix the cauliflower, cheese, flour, yogurt, coriander seeds, garam masala, salt and pepper.

Heat a large, non-stick skillet on medium-high and add the oil until it covers the bottom of the skillet. Roll the cauliflower mixture into balls about the size of golf balls and begin to place them in the heated oil. Fry on all sides until golden brown, 2 to 3 minutes. Remove them as they are cooked and set aside.

FOR THE SAUCE In a second skillet, heat the oil and cook the garlic and ginger on medium-high for 30 seconds. Add the sugar, garam masala, paprika, coriander, cardamom, salt and pepper and cook for 10 seconds. Add the coconut milk and cook for a few minutes to heat through.

Serve the pakoras in the Curry Sauce with rice or rotis. **SERVES 4**

Koftas were cooked on special occasions, especially when my mom's favourite guests came to visit from a far-off village. Once in a while, she cooked them when I would not stop begging for them. She would grate zucchini and add it to chickpeas, and make her village-famous koftas. I have modified her recipe, omitting the zucchini and adding refried beans. The golden colour of the koftas with the green pea sauce makes a beautiful presentation.

Refried Bean Koftas with Pea Sauce

Refried Bean Koftas

1 cup (250 mL) refried beans

½ cup (125 mL) canned chickpeas, rinsed, drained and mashed well

1 small onion, minced

1 green chili, seeds removed and minced

½ cup (125 mL) chickpea flour

1 Tbsp (15 mL) mild curry masala (see page 12)

1 Tbsp (15 mL) coriander seeds

1 Tbsp (15 mL) cumin seeds

1 Tbsp (15 mL) garam masala (see page 11)

1 tsp (5 mL) ground cardamom

pinch of salt and pepper

1 cup (250 mL) grapeseed oil

FOR THE KOFTAS In a medium bowl, thoroughly combine the refried beans, chickpeas, onion, chili, chickpea flour, mild curry masala, coriander, cumin, garam masala, cardamom, salt and pepper.

Form the mixture into small patties, about 2 inches (5 cm) in diameter. Heat the oil in a large skillet on medium heat and begin adding the koftas, frying until they are golden and crispy, about 3 to 5 minutes. Drain on a rack.

Pea Sauce

2 Tbsp (30 mL) grapeseed oil

1 medium onion, chopped

1 Tbsp (15 mL) chopped ginger

1 tsp (5 mL) mustard seeds

*¼ cup (60 mL) loosely packed
fresh curry leaves*

1 Tbsp (15 mL) ground coriander

1 green chili, chopped

2 cups (500 mL) frozen peas

*14 oz (398 mL) can whole
tomatoes, drained*

pinch of saffron

salt and pepper to taste

1 cup (250 mL) vegetable broth

FOR THE PEA SAUCE In a saucepan, cook the oil, onion and ginger on medium-high until the onions begin to brown, about 3 to 5 minutes. Add the mustard seeds then the curry leaves, coriander and the chili and cook for 1 minute, stirring frequently. Add the peas, tomatoes, saffron, salt and pepper then the vegetable broth and bring to a boil. Turn the heat down and simmer, uncovered, until the sauce begins to reduce, about 15 minutes. Turn the heat off.

Let the sauce cool before puréeing in a blender.

TO PLATE THE DISH Place ¾ cup (185 mL) pea sauce in a shallow bowl. Set a few bean koftas on top. Serve with rice or rotis. **SERVES 4**

The only way I used to eat sweet potatoes was cooked over medium-hot coals, which would slowly roast them into sugary-sweet snacks. I always wondered how good they would be if I added some savoury spices. I decided to try sweet potato koftas, which are similar to deep-fried fritters, and combined them with ginger curry. Even I was surprised by the results.

Sweet Potato Koftas with Ginger Curry

Sweet Potato Koftas

2 cups (500 mL) cooked, mashed sweet potatoes

½ cup (125 mL) chickpea flour

¼ cup (60 mL) chopped cilantro

2 Tbsp (30 mL) plain yogurt

1 Tbsp (15 mL) garam masala (see page 11)

1 Tbsp (15 mL) cumin seeds

1 Tbsp (15 mL) grated ginger

1 tsp (5 mL) salt

2 Tbsp (30 mL) grapeseed oil

Ginger Curry

2 Tbsp (30 mL) grapeseed oil

2 Tbsp (30 mL) finely chopped ginger

1 tsp (5 mL) ground ginger

2 Tbsp (30 mL) cumin seeds

1 Tbsp (15 mL) garam masala (see page 11)

1 tsp (5 mL) ground turmeric

salt and pepper to taste

14 oz (398 mL) can coconut milk

FOR THE KOFTAS In a medium bowl, mix the mashed potatoes with the chickpea flour, cilantro, yogurt, garam masala, cumin seeds, ginger and salt. Form the mixture into small patties about 2 inches (5 cm) in diameter.

Heat the oil in a large, non-stick skillet on medium-high. Cook the patties in batches so they have plenty of room to fry, about 2 minutes per side, until they are golden, crispy and cooked through. Remove from the pan and set aside.

FOR THE CURRY Heat the oil in a large saucepan on medium-high. Add the fresh and ground ginger and cook for 30 seconds. Add the cumin seeds, garam masala, turmeric, salt and pepper and cook for about 30 seconds. Add the coconut milk and cook for a few minutes, until heated through.

Pour the Ginger Curry into a serving bowl and gently stir in the koftas.

Serve with rice. **SERVES 4**

Every night in my mother's kitchen she would make lentils. They were easy to digest and I looked forward to eating a different variety each evening. She had several different jars of lentils and I still remember all the flavours. I've put my favourite in this recipe to take you on a journey through my childhood.

Brown Lentils with Mixed Vegetables

2 Tbsp (30 mL) grapeseed oil

2 Tbsp (30 mL) finely chopped ginger

2 Tbsp (30 mL) finely chopped garlic

2 Tbsp (30 mL) cumin seeds

1 Tbsp (15 mL) garam masala (see page 11)

1 tsp (5 mL) ground turmeric

salt and pepper to taste

1 cup (250 mL) brown lentils

1 cup (250 mL) mixed vegetables, such as corn, peas and green beans

Heat the oil in a large saucepan on medium-high. Add the ginger and garlic and cook for 2 minutes. Add the spices, salt and pepper and cook for 2 minutes more. Add the lentils and 6 cups (1.5 L) water and bring to a boil. Turn the heat to low and cook until the lentils are almost cooked, about 35 to 40 minutes.

Add the vegetables and simmer until the lentils are fully cooked, about 5 minutes.

Serve with rice. **SERVES 4**

Every time I cook lentils, I pour them dry onto a large platter and go over each lentil to make sure there is no grit. I find it very meditative and peaceful, and there is nothing worse than biting into grit while savouring your meal. I have noticed, especially with mixed lentils, that there are so many different colours, grit can be easily overlooked. Adding eggplant to this dish was a great idea because its caramelized nutty flavour goes very well with the spices that are infused into the cooked lentils.

Mixed Lentils with Eggplant

2 medium eggplants

1 cup (250 mL) chickpea flour

1 Tbsp (15 mL) garam masala (see page 11)

¼ cup (60 mL) grapeseed oil

1 medium onion, chopped

1 Tbsp (15 mL) crushed garlic

1 Tbsp (15 mL) grated ginger

1 tsp (5 mL) mustard seeds

1 Tbsp (15 mL) spicy curry masala (see page 12)

1 Tbsp (15 mL) smoked paprika

1 tsp (5 mL) ground turmeric

salt and pepper to taste

1 cup (250 mL) mixed lentils

Preheat the grill to medium. Cut the eggplant into ½-inch (1 cm) round slices. In a bowl, add the chickpea flour, garam masala and ¼ cup (60 mL) water. Mix it well. Dip one side of the eggplant slice in the batter and gently place it, dipped-side down, on the greased grill. Cook each side until golden brown, about 6 to 10 minutes per side. Grill the slices on both sides until they are golden brown and soft, about 4 minutes per side. Set them aside.

In a large pot, on medium-high, heat the oil and cook the onion, garlic and ginger for 4 minutes, stirring frequently. Add the mustard seeds and cook for 10 seconds. Turn the heat to medium-low. Add the spicy curry masala, paprika, turmeric, salt and pepper and cook for 30 seconds. Add the lentils and 6 cups (1.5 L) water and bring to a boil. Turn the heat to low and cook until the lentils are done, about 30 to 40 minutes.

Gently stir the eggplant pieces into the lentils.

Serve with rice or rotis. **SERVES 4**

MIXED LENTILS WITH EGGPLANT (RIGHT),
BITTER MELON WITH CARAMELIZED ONIONS
(PAGE 63) (LEFT)

For the longest time I could not remember the name of mung beans. In the village, they were called moongie-di-dahl. *They were considered part of the lentil family, and there were so many different kinds of lentils that I could not remember the names. I started calling them by their colour, but that was frowned upon because in order for a woman to be a good wife she must know the proper names of each lentil. Even though this was one of my favourite lentils, I still struggled with the name. But on the bright side, I was able to master this dish exactly like my great-aunt made it in the village, and here is the recipe for you to share with your family and friends.*

Mung Beans with Grilled Corn

5 corn cobs, husk removed

3 Tbsp (45 mL) grapeseed oil

2 Tbsp (30 mL) coriander seeds

1 Tbsp (15 mL) cumin seeds

1 Tbsp (15 mL) garam masala (see page 11)

1 tsp (5 mL) fenugreek seeds

1 tsp (5 mL) black mustard seeds

1 tsp (5 mL) ground turmeric

¼ cup (60 mL) dried curry leaves

2 Tbsp (30 mL) minced ginger

1 Tbsp (15 mL) minced garlic

salt and pepper to taste

1 large onion, thinly sliced

1 cup (250 mL) mung beans

Barbecue the cobs on medium heat until the kernels are golden brown, about 8 to 10 minutes. Let them cool and then cut off the kernels with a serrated knife.

Heat the oil in a large pot over medium heat. When it is hot, add the coriander seeds, cumin seeds, garam masala, fenugreek seeds, black mustard seeds, turmeric, curry leaves, ginger, garlic, salt and pepper and then the onion. Cook until the onion is tender, about 4 minutes.

Add the mung beans and 7 cups (1.75 L) of water and bring to a boil. Turn down the heat and let simmer until the mung beans are cooked, about 30 to 45 minutes.

Add the corn kernels before serving with rice or rotis.

SERVES 4

Kidney beans are called rajmanh *in Punjabi. My mother made the best rajmanh in the village. She never had access to Italian herb seasoning and often we could not afford even the basic spices such as cumin and fenugreek seeds, but her homemade garam masala was magical and she cooked ginger and garlic to perfection and added tons of love. I tried to bring back those village memories by recreating this recipe.*

Red Kidney Beans with Tomato Sauce

2 Tbsp (30 mL) grapeseed oil

2 Tbsp (30 mL) finely chopped ginger

2 Tbsp (30 mL) finely chopped garlic

2 Tbsp (30 mL) cumin seeds

1 Tbsp (15 mL) garam masala (see page 11)

1 Tbsp (15 mL) Italian herb seasoning

1 tsp (5 mL) fenugreek seeds

1 tsp (5 mL) ground turmeric

salt and pepper to taste

¼ cup (60 mL) tamarind pulp

1 Tbsp (15 mL) brown sugar

14 oz (398 mL) can crushed tomatoes

14 oz (398 mL) can kidney beans, drained

1 cup (250 mL) loosely packed chopped cilantro

Heat the oil in a large saucepan on medium-high, add the ginger and garlic and cook for 2 minutes. Add the spices, salt and pepper, then the tamarind pulp and sugar and cook for about 2 minutes.

Add the crushed tomatoes and 1 cup (250 mL) water and cook for 3 to 4 minutes. Add the kidney beans and cilantro and cook for 2 minutes to heat through. Turn off the heat, cover with a lid and let sit for 10 minutes.

Serve with rice or rotis. **SERVES 4**

I can eat chickpeas for breakfast, lunch and dinner. Especially this recipe! Not only is it very easy, healthy and quick to make but it is also absolutely delicious. After eating it once, you will want it again, I can guarantee that.

Simply Chickpeas

2 Tbsp (30 mL) grapeseed oil

1 Tbsp (15 mL) finely chopped ginger

1 green chili, chopped

¼ cup (60 mL) tamarind sauce

1 Tbsp (15 mL) black cumin seeds

1 Tbsp (15 mL) mild curry masala (see page 12)

1 tsp (5 mL) ground turmeric

salt and pepper to taste

14 oz (398 mL) can chickpeas, drained and rinsed

1 cup (250 mL) diced red onion

In a skillet, heat the oil and cook the ginger and chili on medium heat for 30 seconds. Add the tamarind sauce, black cumin seeds, mild curry masala, turmeric, salt and pepper and cook for 30 seconds. Add the chickpeas and onion and cook until the chickpeas are heated, about 3 to 5 minutes.

Serve with rice or rotis. **SERVES 2 TO 4**

When I first came from India, all of my relatives who lived here in Canada raved about this Canadian dish called Mac and Cheese. They told me it was easy to make and that kids really loved it. When I tried it for the first time, I could not even swallow the first bite. I was not used to eating food from a box. I knew I had to give it a twist. I made this recipe, and now my son, Aaron, and his friends always request it.

Aaron's Mac and Cheese

4 cups (1 L) dried macaroni

3 Tbsp (45 mL) butter

1 onion, minced

2 ripe tomatoes, diced

1 Tbsp (15 mL) mild curry masala (see page 12)

1 tsp (5 mL) ground cumin

1 tsp (5 mL) ground turmeric

½ tsp (2 mL) smoked paprika

¼ tsp (1 mL) ground cardamom

salt and pepper to taste

¼ cup (60 mL) flour

3 cups (750 mL) whole or 2% milk

4 cups (1 L) grated white cheddar

¼ cup (60 mL) dried breadcrumbs

Preheat the oven to 350°F (175°C). Grease a 9- × 13-inch (3.5 L) ovenproof dish with butter.

Fill a large pot with water and a little salt, and bring to a rolling boil on medium-high. Add the macaroni and cook until tender but still firm, 8 to 10 minutes. Drain the macaroni, then put it into the baking dish.

Melt 2 Tbsp (30 mL) of the butter in a large skillet on medium-high heat. Add the onion, and cook until it is just beginning to turn golden, about 3 minutes. Add the tomatoes and spices and cook for 5 minutes. Add salt and pepper to taste, then add the flour and stir for about 2 minutes.

Slowly add the milk and cook for about 15 to 20 minutes, stirring frequently, until the sauce is thick enough to coat the back of a spoon. Add 3 cups (750 mL) of the cheese and stir until melted.

Pour the cheese sauce over the macaroni and stir well so it settles and coats all the macaroni. Sprinkle the top with the remaining cheese and breadcrumbs and bake for 30 minutes, until the top is golden and the macaroni is hot and bubbling. **SERVES 4**

seafood

Scallops with Green Apples and Basil / 83

Mussels with Tomato Curry / 84

Prawns Cooked in Coconut Sauce / 85

Fenugreek Prawns on Crab Cakes with Blue Cheese Sauce / 86

Red Snapper with Spiced Papaya and Pine Nut Salsa / 89

Snapper and Yam with Grilled Beans / 91

Cod with Saffron Edamame Sauce and Kale Chips / 92

Cubed Halibut with Coconut Milk Curry / 94

Spiced Halibut on Yellow Lentil Purée / 95

Salmon and Coconut Okra with Cardamom Pesto / 96

The Fabulous Salmon Burger / 98

Poached Salmon with Mango-Cherry Salsa / 99

Salmon with Parsley and Tomato Sauce / 100

Spiced Cornmeal-Crusted Salmon with Tomato Curry / 101

What I love about scallops is that they are quick to make and they absorb the flavours of spices thoroughly. The tartness of the green apple and the gorgeous aromas of the sage make this dish irresistible.

Scallops with Green Apples and Basil

3 Tbsp (45 mL) grapeseed oil

12 medium scallops

salt and pepper to taste

2 Tbsp (30 mL) butter

1 Tbsp (15 mL) chopped ginger

2 green grapeseed apples, peeled, cored and thinly sliced

1 Tbsp (15 mL) garam masala (see page 11)

1 Tbsp (15 mL) coriander seeds, crushed

1 tsp (5 mL) smoked paprika

salt and pepper to taste

1 cup (250 mL) apple cider

½ cup (125 mL) coconut milk

1 small bunch fresh basil leaves, stems removed

Heat the oil in a large skillet on medium heat. Add the scallops, season with salt and pepper and sauté until they are cooked through, about 3 to 5 minutes. Remove from the pan and keep warm.

Add the butter to the scallop pan. When it begins to foam, add the ginger then the apple slices. Turn the heat to low and cook until the apples are caramelized, about 10 minutes, stirring to break up the apple chunks.

Add the spices, salt and pepper and cook for 1 minute. Pour in the apple cider and cook until the sauce is reduced by one-third, about 10 minutes. Pour in the coconut milk, stir well and continue to reduce until it is thick enough to coat the back of a spoon, about 3 to 5 minutes.

Add the scallops to the pan and stir to heat through. At the last minute, stir in the basil leaves until they are just wilted.

Garnish with fresh basil sprigs and serve with rice.

SERVES 4

I think Anoop was about seven or eight when she suddenly expanded her palate to seafood, and she can eat mussels for breakfast, lunch and dinner. This simple dish is enhanced by the tomatoes and wonderful flavours of the spices. The broth is my favourite part, as it is filled with aromas to entice all palates.

Mussels with Tomato Curry

2 onions, peeled and sliced

6 garlic cloves, peeled

2-inch (5 cm) piece ginger, sliced

1 green chili

¼ cup (60 mL) grapeseed oil

1 Tbsp (15 mL) cumin seeds

1 Tbsp (15 mL) coriander seeds

1 Tbsp (15 mL) garam masala (see page 11)

1 tsp (5 mL) ground turmeric

¼ cup (60 mL) fenugreek leaves

salt and pepper to taste

¼ cup (60 mL) tomato paste

2 cups (500 mL) chicken broth

14 oz (398 mL) can coconut milk

1 cup (250 mL) dry white wine

½ cup (125 mL) crushed tomatoes

¼ cup (60 mL) loosely packed finely chopped cilantro leaves

2 lb (1 kg) black mussels, scrubbed and debearded

In a food processor, blend the onions, garlic, ginger and chili.

In a large saucepan, heat the oil and cook the onion paste on medium-high, stirring frequently, until the paste begins to turn light brown, around 5 to 7 minutes. Add the cumin seeds, coriander seeds, garam masala and turmeric then the fenugreek leaves, salt and pepper and cook for 2 minutes. Add the tomato paste and cook for 1 minute. Add the broth, coconut milk, wine, crushed tomatoes and cilantro then the mussels and cook until the mussels open, about 8 to 10 minutes. Discard any unopened mussels.

To serve, scoop the mussels into a serving bowl and pour the cooking juices over them. Serve with My Mother's Okra with Sautéed Tomatoes (page 64) and rice. **SERVES 4**

Spices and seafood are a marriage made in heaven. In this recipe, the spices not only add their uniqueness to the prawns but also enhance the coconut sauce. The mint and cilantro make the sauce a beautiful green colour that looks lovely with the seared prawns.

Prawns Cooked in Coconut Sauce

2 Tbsp (30 mL) grapeseed oil

1 Tbsp (15 mL) grated garlic

1 tsp (5 mL) fenugreek leaves

1 tsp (5 mL) smoked paprika

1 tsp (5 mL) cumin seeds

¼ tsp (1 mL) cardamom seeds

8 large prawns, peeled and deveined

1 cup (250 mL) loosely packed chopped mint leaves

1 cup (250 mL) loosely packed cilantro leaves

salt and pepper to taste

14 oz (398 mL) can coconut milk

1 Tbsp (15 mL) lime juice

Heat the oil in a skillet on medium-high. Add the garlic, fenugreek, paprika, cumin and cardamom seeds and toast until the garlic is golden, about 30 seconds. Add the prawns, mint, cilantro, salt and pepper, and cook for 1 minute.

Add the coconut milk and cook until the prawns are firm and curled up, about 4 to 6 minutes. Add the lime juice and turn off the heat.

Serve warm with rice or rotis. **SERVES 4**

This recipe came to my mind when I had a few ingredients lying around in the fridge. I created crab cakes from left-over crab after making sushi the day before. What I love about this dish is that it easily comes together to make a striking arrangement on the plate.

Fenugreek Prawns on Crab Cakes with Blue Cheese Sauce

Blue Cheese Sauce

½ tsp (2 mL) brown mustard seeds

1 cup (250 mL) sour cream

1 cup (250 mL) mayonnaise

4 oz (125 g) blue cheese, crumbled

2 garlic cloves, crushed

½ tsp (2 mL) red chili flakes

¼ tsp (1 mL) ground mustard

salt and pepper to taste

Crab Cakes

1 egg

8 oz (250 g) crabmeat

1 small red onion, minced

½ cup (125 mL) crushed crackers

2 Tbsp (30 mL) dried fenugreek leaves

1 Tbsp (15 mL) garam masala (see page 11)

1 tsp (5 mL) ground turmeric

zest of 1 lemon

2 Tbsp (30 mL) grapeseed oil

FOR THE BLUE CHEESE SAUCE Heat a small skillet on low and toast the mustard seeds for 15 to 20 seconds, until they start popping. Remove from the heat. In a bowl, thoroughly whisk all the sauce ingredients together.

FOR THE CRAB CAKES In a bowl, whisk the egg, then add the rest of the ingredients, except the oil, and mix well.

Heat the oil in a non-stick skillet on medium-high. Shape the crab mixture into 4 patties and gently place them in the skillet. Cook for 6 to 8 minutes per side, until they are golden brown. Set aside and keep warm.

RECIPE CONTINUES ON NEXT PAGE . . .

Fenugreek Prawns on Crab Cakes with Blue Cheese Sauce

(CONTINUED)

Fenugreek Prawns

2 Tbsp (30 mL) grapeseed oil

1 Tbsp (15 mL) chopped garlic

1 red chili

1 tsp (5 mL) coriander seeds

¼ cup (60 mL) dried fenugreek leaves

salt and pepper to taste

12 large tiger prawns, peeled and deveined, but with the tail still on

FOR THE PRAWNS In a skillet, cook the oil and garlic on medium-high until the garlic is cooked, about 2 minutes. Add the chili and coriander seeds, then the fenugreek leaves, salt and pepper and cook for 30 seconds. Add the prawns and cook, stirring frequently, until the prawns are firm, about 2 minutes.

TO PLATE THE DISH Put a few tablespoons of Blue Cheese Sauce on a plate, gently top with a crab cake and finish with 3 tiger prawns. **SERVES 4**

SUGGESTED WINE
2011 Viognier by Moraine Winery

Snapper is a very easy, quick fish to cook. Fresh papaya salsa with toasted pine nuts not only makes this dish flavourful but also creates a beautiful presentation to impress your guests. It is very simple to toast pine nuts and they give a wonderful nutty flavour to the dish. I toast them in a heavy pan on medium-low for a few minutes and stir them often so they don't burn.

Red Snapper with Spiced Papaya and Pine Nut Salsa

Snapper

2 Tbsp (30 mL) grapeseed oil

1 Tbsp (15 mL) ground coriander

1 tsp (5 mL) smoked paprika

salt and pepper to taste

four 6 oz (175 g) red snapper fillets

Papaya and Pine Nut Salsa

1 medium papaya, peeled, seeded and cubed

1 small red onion, finely chopped

¼ cup (60 mL) loosely packed thinly chopped basil

¼ cup (60 mL) toasted pine nuts

1 Tbsp (15 mL) lemon juice

¼ tsp (1 mL) lemon zest

salt and pepper to taste

TO PREPARE THE SNAPPER Heat the oil in a non-stick skillet on medium-high. Mix together the coriander, paprika, salt and pepper and rub the fish with the mixture. Gently place the fillets in the skillet. Cook on each side for 3 to 4 minutes, until just cooked.

TO PREPARE THE SALSA Combine the papaya, onion, basil, pine nuts, lemon juice and zest, salt and pepper in a bowl.

TO PLATE THE DISH Place a fillet on a plate and add a large dollop of salsa before serving. **SERVES 4**

My love for yams inspired me to create this recipe. Snapper does not have much flavour on its own, but when it's combined with spices and layers of yam, it becomes a divine dish. I decided to add the green beans because not only do they add nutrition to the meal, they also make the dish delicious and beautiful.

Snapper and Yam with Grilled Beans

Pan-fried Snapper and Yam

four 6 oz (175 g) snapper fillets

1 Tbsp (15 mL) ground coriander

¼ tsp (1 mL) smoked paprika

salt and pepper to taste

1 yam, peeled, and sliced thinly, crosswise

2 Tbsp (30 mL) grapeseed oil

Grilled Beans

2 Tbsp (30 mL) grapeseed oil

2 Tbsp (30 mL) garam masala (see page 11)

salt and pepper to taste

1 lb (500 g) green beans

lemon wedges for garnish

FOR THE SNAPPER Sprinkle one side of the snapper fillets with coriander, paprika, salt and pepper. Gently press a few yam slices onto each spiced fillet.

In a skillet, heat the oil on medium-high. Gently place the fillet yam side down in the skillet and cook until the yam begins to brown, about 3 minutes. Gently flip the fillet over and cook until the fish can be flaked with a fork, about 3 to 5 minutes.

FOR THE BEANS In a bowl, combine the oil, garam masala, salt and pepper. Heat the grill to medium-high and brush the spiced oil on the beans. Gently place them on the grill and cook until the beans are tender, with a nice golden brown colour on all sides, about 4 to 6 minutes.

TO PLATE THE DISH Arrange one-quarter of the grilled beans on a plate. Gently place a snapper fillet on the beans, yam side up. Garnish with lemon wedges.

SERVES 4

||||||||||||||||||||||||||||||||||||||||||||

SUGGESTED WINE

2011 Pinot Gris by Perseus Winery

When I am making a sauce that already has pungent flavours, I usually use cheap saffron, which has a very light colour and can be purchased from any grocery store. It still gives a hint of saffron and that's all you need for this edamame sauce. This quick recipe lets you spend more time with your guests than in the kitchen.

Cod with Saffron Edamame Sauce and Kale Chips

Cod

2 Tbsp (30 mL) grapeseed oil

four 6 oz (175 g) cod fillets

1 Tbsp (15 mL) seafood masala (see page 10)

salt and pepper to taste

Edamame Sauce

2 Tbsp (30 mL) grapeseed oil

1 medium onion, chopped

1 Tbsp (15 mL) chopped ginger

1 tsp (5 mL) brown mustard seeds

¼ cup (60 mL) loosely packed fresh curry leaves

1 Tbsp (15 mL) ground coriander

1 green chili, chopped (leave in the seeds if you like the heat)

2 cups (500 mL) vegetable broth

2 cups (500 mL) frozen edamame beans

14 oz (398 mL) can whole tomatoes, drained

pinch of saffron

salt and pepper to taste

TO PREPARE THE COD In a large skillet, heat the oil on medium-high. Sprinkle both sides of the cod with the seafood masala, salt and pepper. Gently place the fillets in the skillet and cook until they flake easily with a fork, about 3 minutes per side.

Remove the cod from the skillet and set aside.

TO PREPARE THE SAUCE Cook the oil, onion and ginger in a large saucepan on medium-high until the onion begins to brown, about 3 to 5 minutes. Add the mustard seeds then the curry leaves, coriander and chili and cook for 1 minute, stirring frequently. Add the broth, edamame beans, tomatoes, saffron, salt and pepper and bring to a boil. Turn down the heat and simmer, uncovered, until the sauce begins to reduce, about 10 minutes. Let the sauce cool slightly before puréeing the tomatoes with a hand blender.

Kale Chips

6-8 kale leaves

2 Tbsp (30 mL) grapeseed oil

*½ tsp (2 mL) garam masala
(see page 11)*

¼ tsp (1 mL) smoked paprika

salt and pepper to taste

FOR THE KALE CHIPS Preheat the oven to 325°F (160°C). Wash and gently towel dry the kale leaves, then tear off the thick stems and discard them. Place the leaves on a baking sheet. Mix the oil and spices in a bowl and brush the leaves with it. Bake until the leaves are golden brown and crispy, about 15 minutes. Let them cool and break them into chips before serving.

TO PLATE THE DISH Place a few tablespoons of edamame sauce on a plate and gently place a cod fillet on the sauce. Garnish with kale chips. **SERVES 4**

Pan-frying is the best way to cook fish, and I like to prepare it separately from the sauce. This way, you can retain the crunchiness of the fish. In this recipe, I enjoy cooking with coconut milk because it gives a nice creamy texture to the sauce, complementing the creamy texture of the halibut. This is a common dish in my kitchen, and it is simple, quick and healthy.

Cubed Halibut with Coconut Milk Curry

Halibut

2 Tbsp (30 mL) grapeseed oil

1 Tbsp (15 mL) butter

1 Tbsp (15 mL) ground coriander

two 6 oz (175 g) halibut fillets, cubed

Coconut Milk Curry

2 Tbsp (30 mL) grapeseed oil

1 tsp (5 mL) crushed garlic

¼ cup (60 mL) loosely packed fresh curry leaves

1 Tbsp (15 mL) ground coriander

1 tsp (5 mL) brown mustard seeds

1 tsp (5 mL) smoked paprika

salt and pepper to taste

14 oz (398 mL) can coconut milk

TO PREPARE THE HALIBUT In a skillet, heat the oil and butter on medium-high until the butter begins to turn light brown. Sprinkle the ground coriander on the halibut, add it to the pan and cook for about 3 minutes, stirring gently and frequently. Set it aside.

FOR THE CURRY In another skillet, cook the oil and garlic on medium-high for 2 minutes. Add the curry leaves, coriander, mustard seeds, paprika, salt and pepper and cook for 30 seconds. Add the coconut milk and cook until the liquid begins to thicken, about 3 to 5 minutes.

Gently place the halibut in the sauce.

Serve with rice or quinoa. **SERVES 4**

I really enjoy this recipe. Both of the main ingredients, halibut and lentils, have amazing health benefits. I use split lentils here because they don't take long to cook compared to full-seeded lentils that can take forever. I like to make a thick purée so the fish sits nicely on it. A green garnish on the fish, either a thin slice of lime or a few pieces of cilantro, makes this entire dish look even better.

Spiced Halibut on Yellow Lentil Purée

Yellow Lentil Purée

1 cup (250 mL) yellow split lentils

1 Tbsp (15 mL) ground coriander

1 tsp (5 mL) ground turmeric

salt and pepper to taste

Spiced Halibut

four 6 oz (175 g) halibut fillets

1 Tbsp (15 mL) garam masala (see page 11)

salt and pepper to taste

¼ cup (60 mL) flour

¼ cup (60 mL) grapeseed oil

1 Tbsp (15 mL) butter

FOR THE PURÉE Combine all the purée ingredients in a large saucepan with 4 cups (1 L) water and cook, uncovered, on medium heat until the lentils are done, about 20 to 25 minutes. Turn off the heat.

FOR THE HALIBUT Sprinkle both sides of each fillet with garam masala, salt and pepper and lightly dredge in the flour. Shake off the excess flour.

In a non-stick skillet, heat the oil and butter on medium until the butter begins to brown a little. Add the fillets and cook until they are almost done, about 2 to 3 minutes per side.

TO PLATE THE DISH Place a few tablespoons of lentil purée on the plate and then gently place a fillet on top. SERVES 4

SUGGESTED WINE

2010 Pinot Noir by Howling Bluff Estate Wines

I often wondered what pesto would taste like if I added a few green cardamom seeds. I was pleasantly surprised by how the pungent flavour of basil complemented the floral flavour of cardamom. This sauce works well with any seafood. I have served scallops and prawns with it and enjoyed it very much. In this recipe, the salmon takes in all the amazing flavours of the spices and beautifully complements the cardamom in the pesto sauce. A little spoonful of pesto goes a long way.

Salmon and Coconut Okra with Cardamom Pesto

Coconut Okra

2 Tbsp (30 mL) grapeseed oil

1 tsp (5 mL) grated ginger

1 lb (500 g) okra, hard ends removed and cut in half lengthwise

1 tsp (5 mL) fennel seeds

1 tsp (5 mL) ground coriander

½ tsp (2 mL) brown mustard seeds

½ tsp (2 mL) cardamom seeds

½ tsp (2 mL) ground cardamom

salt and pepper to taste

14 oz (398 mL) can coconut milk

Grilled Salmon

four 6 oz (175 g) salmon steaks

FOR THE OKRA Cook the oil and ginger in a skillet on medium-high for 2 to 3 minutes, until the ginger is soft. Add the okra and cook until golden brown, about 6 to 8 minutes. Add the spices and cook for 1 minute. Add the coconut milk and cook, uncovered, until reduced by half, about 6 to 8 minutes. Keep warm.

FOR THE SALMON Preheat the grill to medium. Grill the salmon steaks until they can be flaked with a fork, turning once, about 10 to 12 minutes.

FOR THE PESTO While the salmon is cooking, prepare the pesto. Toast the pine nuts in a heavy pan on medium-low for a few minutes, stirring often. In a food processor, combine the pine nuts, basil, olive oil, paneer, cardamom, smoked paprika, salt and pepper until they turn into a smooth paste.

TO PLATE THE DISH Put a few tablespoons of Coconut Okra on a plate. Gently place a salmon steak on the okra and top with a spoonful of Cardamom Pesto. **SERVES 4**

Cardamom Pesto

¼ cup (60 mL) pine nuts

2 cups (500 mL) basil

½ cup (125 mL) olive oil

½ cup (125 mL) paneer (see page 51)

1 tsp (5 mL) ground cardamom

¼ tsp (1 mL) smoked paprika

salt and pepper to taste

The Fabulous Salmon Burger

two 6 oz (175 g) salmon fillets, deboned and finely chopped

1 small red onion, finely chopped

1 green chili, finely chopped (include seeds if you want it really spicy)

1 cup (250 mL) fenugreek leaves, finely chopped

1 Tbsp (15 mL) ground coriander

1 tsp (5 mL) cumin seeds

salt and pepper to taste

2 Tbsp (30 mL) grapeseed oil

In a bowl, thoroughly combine all the ingredients, except the oil until the mixture holds together and can be shaped. If you can't fully mix the salmon, give the mixture a quick pulse in a food processor to shred the fish.

Preheat the grill to medium-high and brush with the oil. Shape the salmon mixture into 4 patties. Gently place them on the grill. Once one side is golden brown, about 4 minutes, gently flip the burger and grill until the salmon is cooked through, about 4 minutes more.

Serve in buns with your favourite toppings. **SERVES 4**

For this recipe I use sockeye salmon. When I added the basmati rice (see My Everyday Rice, page 135) and the sweet flavours of this salsa, I satisfied every single taste bud in my mouth. I don't crave dessert after this recipe.

Poached Salmon with Mango-Cherry Salsa

Poached Salmon

1 cup (250 mL) dry white wine

1 cup (250 mL) clam juice

6 whole star anise

two 4 inch (10 cm) cinnamon sticks

6 bay leaves

four 6 oz (175 g) salmon fillets

1 tsp (5 mL) garam masala (see page 11)

1 tsp (5 mL) lemon zest

Mango-Cherry Salsa

1 small red onion, diced

1 large ripe mango, peeled, pitted and cubed

1 cup (250 mL) pitted cherries, halved

¼ cup (60 mL) red wine balsamic vinegar

1 tsp (5 mL) ground fennel

½ tsp (2 mL) ground cardamom

juice of 1 lemon

salt and pepper to taste

4 cups (1 L) My Everyday Rice (page 135)

FOR THE SALMON Heat the wine, clam juice, star anise, cinnamon sticks and bay leaves in a large non-stick skillet on low heat. Gently place the salmon fillets in the poaching liquid. Sprinkle garam masala and lemon zest on each fillet. Cover the skillet and reduce the heat to low. Poach until the salmon is firm, about 13 to 15 minutes.

FOR THE SALSA Gently toss the onion, mango, cherries, vinegar, fennel, cardamom, lemon juice, salt and pepper in a large bowl.

TO PLATE THE DISH Place 1 cup (250 mL) of rice on a plate, gently place a salmon fillet on the rice, and top with 2 tablespoons (30 mL) of salsa. **SERVES 4**

It is a blessing to live on the west coast because I have access to fresh fish such as salmon. I enjoy combining coconut milk in the sauce to give it a richer flavour.

Salmon with Parsley and Tomato Sauce

Salmon with Parsley

3 Tbsp (45 mL) grapeseed oil

1 Tbsp (15 mL) butter

½ cup (125 mL) finely chopped parsley

2 Tbsp (30 mL) Italian seasoning

1 Tbsp (15 mL) garam masala (see page 11)

salt and pepper to taste

four 6 oz (175 g) salmon fillets

Tomato Sauce

2 Tbsp (30 mL) grapeseed oil

1 Tbsp (15 mL) chopped garlic

½ tsp (2 mL) ground coriander

½ tsp (2 mL) smoked paprika

½ tsp (2 mL) fennel seeds

salt and pepper to taste

1 lb (500 g) cherry tomatoes

FOR THE SALMON In a skillet on medium heat, heat the oil and butter until the butter browns. Mix the parsley, Italian seasoning, garam masala, salt and pepper in a bowl. With your hands, press the mixture into the skinless side of the salmon. Place the salmon parsley side down in the skillet and cook for 3 to 4 minutes. Gently flip the salmon with a spatula and cook until the salmon can be flaked with a fork, about 4 to 6 minutes.

FOR THE SAUCE Cook the oil and garlic in a saucepan on medium-high until the garlic is golden brown. Add the coriander, paprika, fennel seeds, salt and pepper then the tomatoes and cook, stirring frequently, until the tomatoes are soft, about 6 to 8 minutes. Let it cool, then purée the mixture in a food processor. Reheat the sauce before serving.

TO PLATE THE DISH Spread a few tablespoons of Tomato Sauce on a plate and gently place a salmon fillet on top.

SERVES 4

I look for different techniques to cook salmon and this is one of my favourites. I add the gorgeous flavours of spices in the cornmeal before dipping the salmon fillets in it. This way, when you take a bite of the crusted salmon, it is filled with the great spice flavours. In this recipe, I use a tomato curry, but you can also try coconut milk to give it an even richer taste.

Spiced Cornmeal-Crusted Salmon with Tomato Curry

1 cup (250 mL) fine cornmeal

1 tsp (5 mL) ground coriander

1 tsp (5 mL) ground cardamom

½ tsp (2 mL) smoked paprika

salt and pepper to taste

four 6 oz (175 g) skinless salmon fillets

4 Tbsp (60 mL) grapeseed oil

1 medium onion, finely chopped

1 Tbsp (15 mL) finely chopped ginger

1 Tbsp (15 mL) fennel seeds

1 Tbsp (15 mL) cumin seeds

salt and pepper to taste

¼ cup (60 mL) tomato paste

one 19 oz (540 mL) can (about 2 cups/500 mL) crushed tomatoes

basil for garnishing

On a large plate, mix together the cornmeal, coriander, cardamom, paprika, salt and pepper. Coat both sides of the salmon fillets well with the spiced cornmeal.

In a non-stick skillet, heat 2 Tbsp (30 mL) of the oil on medium heat. Gently place the salmon in the pan and cook until done, about 5 minutes per side.

In a saucepan, heat the remaining 2 Tbsp (30 mL) of oil on medium-high. Add the onion and ginger and cook until the onion is tender, about 3 to 5 minutes. Add the fennel seeds, cumin seeds, salt and pepper and cook for 2 minutes. Add the tomato paste and cook for 2 minutes. Add the crushed tomatoes and ¼ cup (60 mL) water and cook on low heat for 5 minutes.

TO PLATE THE DISH Place a few tablespoons of tomato curry in a shallow bowl and gently place the salmon on top. Garnish with fresh basil. **SERVES 4**

eggs, chicken
& meat

In India, when a few of my girlfriends would bring egg curry for lunch, the entire lunch area would fill with delicious curry flavours. In my family, eating eggs was frowned upon, but I wanted to make this dish anyway, using spices from my mother's pantry. Here is the recipe I made when I sneaked out of my house one afternoon and made the egg curry at my friend's house.

Egg Curry with Rapini and Tomatoes

6 medium eggs

2 Tbsp (30 mL) grapeseed oil

1 Tbsp (15 mL) finely chopped ginger

1 Tbsp (15 mL) spicy curry masala (see page 12)

1 tsp (5 mL) ground turmeric

1 tsp (5 mL) ground fennel seed

salt and pepper to taste

1 lb (500 g) fresh rapini, chopped

1 cup (250 mL) quartered cherry tomatoes

Gently place the eggs in a saucepan and add enough water to cover them. Bring to a boil on medium-high and boil until the eggs are fully cooked, about 5 minutes. Remove from the heat and allow the eggs to cool, then peel off the shells.

In a wide, shallow pan, heat the oil on medium-high. Add the ginger and cook for 15 seconds. Add the spices, salt and pepper and stir to toast for about 10 seconds. Add the rapini and tomatoes and cook for 5 minutes.

Slice the boiled eggs in half and gently stir into the rapini mixture.

Serve with rice. **SERVES 4**

My No-Butter Chicken became one of the top-searched recipes on the Food Network and the U.S. Cooking Channel when my TV show Spice Goddess *was launched in North America. This recipe is inspired by the original recipe, and you will not only love how fabulous it looks but will also fall in love with the flavours all over again.*

Grilled Chicken with No-Butter Sauce

2 Tbsp (30 mL) grapeseed oil

1 onion, chopped

2 Tbsp (30 mL) grated ginger

2 Tbsp (30 mL) chopped garlic

¼ cup (60 mL) dried curry leaves

1 Tbsp (15 mL) brown mustard seeds

1 Tbsp (15 mL) tandoori masala (see page 11)

1 tsp (5 mL) red chili powder

1 tsp (5 mL) ground turmeric

¼ cup (60 mL) tomato paste

2 cups (500 mL) chopped tomatoes

1 cup (250 mL) plain yogurt

4 boneless, skinless chicken breasts

1 Tbsp (15 mL) garam masala (see page 11)

cilantro for garnish

In a large skillet, heat the oil on medium-high. Add the onion, ginger and garlic and cook for 4 minutes, until the onion is soft and golden. Add the curry leaves and spices to the pan and cook for 2 minutes. Add the tomato paste and cook for 1 minute. Add the tomatoes, yogurt and 1 cup (250 mL) of water, turn down the heat to low and cook, uncovered, until the sauce thickens, about 15 minutes.

Preheat the grill to medium-high. Sprinkle the chicken breasts with garam masala and grill on both sides until fully cooked, about 12 to 15 minutes.

Put a few tablespoons of sauce in a shallow bowl and gently place a chicken breast on top. Garnish with cilantro. **SERVES 4**

Because of my love and passion for mango, I decided to incorporate it into this recipe. The warm earthy flavours from the cumin seeds combine very well with the mango's sweetness.

Chicken with Cashews and Mango Sauce

2 Tbsp (30 mL) grapeseed oil

2 Tbsp (30 mL) grated garlic

1 Tbsp (15 mL) grated ginger

1 Tbsp (15 mL) cumin seeds

2 tsp (10 mL) ground coriander

1 tsp (5 mL) fenugreek seeds

1 tsp (5 mL) smoked paprika

½ cup (125 mL) cashews

2 boneless, skinless chicken breasts, cubed

½ cup (125 mL) plain yogurt

2 cups (500 mL) mango chunks

Heat the oil in a large skillet on medium-high. Add the garlic and ginger and sauté for about 1 minute. Add the spices then the cashews and toast for 10 seconds. Turn down the heat to low and add the chicken. Cook until it is nearly done, about 8 minutes.

Add the yogurt and finish cooking the chicken, about 2 more minutes, then stir in the mango chunks.

Serve with rice or rotis. **SERVES 4**

SUGGESTED WINE

2009 Merlot Reserve by Mission Hill Family Estate

Since spinach has such great health benefits, I often make it for lunches for the family. Recently, I started enhancing the flavours by adding chicken and peas for a dinner entrée. My guests can never get enough of it. It would make a wonderful leftover lunch for the next day, but I haven't tried it because in my house there is never enough left to save.

Chicken with Spinach and Peas

2 Tbsp (30 mL) grapeseed oil

1 red onion, chopped

2 Tbsp (30 mL) grated garlic

2 Tbsp (30 mL) grated ginger

1 Tbsp (15 mL) cumin seeds

¼ cup (60 mL) loosely packed fresh curry leaves

1 Tbsp (15 mL) mild curry masala (see page 12)

1 tsp (5 mL) ground turmeric

salt and pepper to taste

2 boneless, skinless chicken breasts, cubed

2 cups (500 mL) chopped tomatoes

2 cups (500 mL) frozen spinach, thawed and water squeezed out

1 cup (250 mL) frozen peas

Heat the oil in a skillet on medium. Add the onion, garlic and ginger and cook until the onion is tender, 3 to 5 minutes.

Add the cumin seeds then the curry leaves, mild curry masala, turmeric, salt and pepper and cook for 30 seconds. Add the chicken cubes and cook until they are almost done, about 5 to 7 minutes. Add the tomatoes, spinach and peas and continue cooking until the chicken is fully cooked and the spices are well combined with the spinach and peas, about 8 to 10 minutes.

Serve with rotis or rice. **SERVES 4**

Chicken thighs have juicy, tender meat that is actually my favourite meat. I decided to add coconut milk to this recipe because it adds a very nice creaminess and refreshing flavours. Try adding fresh coconut flakes for additional flavour and texture.

Chicken Thighs in Coconut Masala

2 Tbsp (30 mL) grapeseed oil

2 Tbsp (30 mL) finely chopped garlic

2 Tbsp (30 mL) finely chopped ginger

1 green chili, finely chopped

1 Tbsp (15 mL) mild curry masala (see page 12)

1 Tbsp (15 mL) coriander seeds

1 tsp (5 mL) fenugreek seeds

salt and pepper to taste

1 Tbsp (15 mL) tomato paste

6 chicken thighs, skin on

2 onions, sliced

2 ripe tomatoes, diced

1 cup (250 mL) chicken broth

14 oz (398 mL) can coconut milk

Heat the oil in a large saucepan on medium-high. Add the garlic, ginger and chili and sauté for 30 seconds. Add the spices, salt and pepper and toast for 10 seconds, then add the tomato paste. Stir well, add the chicken and onions and cook for a few minutes until the onions are tender.

Add the tomatoes, broth and coconut milk. Bring to a boil, then reduce the heat to a simmer. Cover and cook for about 20 to 25 minutes, until the chicken is cooked through.

Serve with rice. **SERVES 4**

This is a perfect patio dish to make for your guests and family. If there are leftovers, I add them to a wrap for the next day's lunch. Sometimes I serve the chicken skewers as appetizers with chutney.

Mint Chicken with Coconut Rice

Mint Chicken

2 boneless, skinless chicken breasts, cubed

½ cup (125 mL) finely chopped mint leaves

2 Tbsp (30 mL) tamarind pulp

1 Tbsp (15 mL) grated ginger

1 Tbsp (15 mL) brown sugar

1 Tbsp (15 mL) garam masala (see page 11)

pinch of salt

4 metal or bamboo skewers (see note)

oil for the grill

Coconut Rice

2 cups (500 mL) long-grain rice

2 cups (500 mL) water

1 cup (250 mL) coconut milk

1 Tbsp (15 mL) garam masala

½ tsp (2 mL) red chili flakes

salt and pepper to taste

FOR THE CHICKEN In a large bowl, combine the chicken, mint, tamarind, ginger, sugar, garam masala and salt. Cover and marinate in the fridge for 30 minutes to 2 hours.

Preheat the grill to medium-high. Thread the chicken cubes onto the skewers and brush oil on the grill. Grill the skewers, turning frequently and basting with the remaining marinade, for about 7 to 8 minutes per side, until the chicken juices run clear. Cut a piece of chicken open with a small knife to test for doneness.

TO MAKE THE COCONUT RICE In a saucepan, combine all the ingredients and bring to a boil. Turn the heat to low, cover and cook until the rice is done, about 20 to 30 minutes.

TO PLATE THE DISH Spoon the Coconut Rice onto a dish. Arrange the chicken skewers overtop. **SERVES 4**

NOTE
If using bamboo skewers, soak them in water for a few hours before using.

Punjabi stews are called sabjis, *and are my all-time favourite food. I love how the spices slowly cook for hours and are totally infused into the vegetables or meats. If you visit my house during cold fall days, you will see this stew often on my weekly menu. What I love about this recipe is that you can prepare it in the morning and have time for other chores during the rest of the day, and it's all ready for dinner. The meat just melts in your mouth.*

Chicken Sabji

2 Tbsp (30 mL) grapeseed oil

1 Tbsp (15 mL) mild curry masala (see page 12)

1 tsp (5 mL) smoked paprika

1 tsp (5 mL) ground coriander

½ tsp (2 mL) ground cardamom

1 Tbsp (15 mL) brown sugar

salt and pepper to taste

4 boneless, skinless chicken breasts, cubed

1 onion, chopped

1 Tbsp (15 mL) chopped garlic

1 Tbsp (15 mL) chopped ginger

2 medium carrots, diced

2 celery stalks, diced

1 cup (250 mL) chicken broth

In a skillet, heat the oil and add the spices then the sugar, salt and pepper on medium heat and cook for 20 seconds. Add the chicken and cook for about 3 to 5 minutes, until the chicken is nicely coated with the spices. Add the onion, garlic and ginger and cook for another minute.

Add the carrots, celery and chicken broth and cook, stirring occasionally, until the chicken is fully cooked, about 8 to 10 minutes.

Serve with rotis or rice. **SERVES 4**

When you think of tandoori chicken, you picture the gorgeous red colour of the sauce. Frequently, that colour comes from food colouring. I've achieved the same colour by adding sweet smoked paprika, which gives a rich red colour and does not have much heat to it.

Tandoori Baked Chicken

1 cup (250 mL) plain yogurt

1 clove garlic, crushed

¼ cup (60 mL) tomato paste

¼ cup (60 mL) dried fenugreek leaves

2 Tbsp (30 mL) tandoori masala (see page 11)

1 Tbsp (15 mL) garam masala (see page 11)

½ Tbsp (7.5 mL) brown sugar

4 chicken legs, split into thighs and drumsticks

Thoroughly combine all the ingredients except the chicken legs in a large bowl. Set aside ¼ cup (60 mL) for basting. Add the chicken pieces and stir to coat well. Cover the bowl and marinate in the fridge for 45 minutes to 4 hours.

Preheat the grill to medium-high and oil the grill. Remove the chicken from the marinade and grill, turning and basting frequently with the reserved marinade, until the chicken is done and the juices run clear, about 35 to 40 minutes.

Serve with rice. **SERVES 4**

‖‖‖‖‖‖‖‖‖‖‖‖‖‖‖‖‖‖‖‖‖‖‖‖‖‖‖‖‖‖‖‖‖‖‖‖

SUGGESTED WINE
2011 Monster Cabs by Monster Vineyards

TANDOORI BAKED CHICKEN AND
MY EVERYDAY RICE (PAGE 135)
(BOTTOM), PAN-FRIED ZUCCHINI
WITH CILANTRO COCONUT SAUCE
(PAGE 60) (TOP)

This chicken and kidney beans dish is so easy to make, and after eating it once, I promise you will want to eat it again and again. Cardamom and fennel seeds are often added to desserts, but I added them to the savoury flavours in this recipe to create this mouth-watering dish that both of my kids constantly request for dinner.

Chicken and Kidney Beans

2 Tbsp (30 mL) grapeseed oil

1 large onion, finely chopped

2 Tbsp (30 mL) finely chopped garlic

2 Tbsp (30 mL) finely chopped ginger

1 green chili, finely chopped

1 Tbsp (15 mL) garam masala (see page 11)

1 tsp (5 mL) smoked paprika

1 tsp (5 mL) ground turmeric

salt to taste

4 chicken legs, split into thighs and drumsticks

2 cups (500 mL) chopped tomatoes

¼ cup (60 mL) loosely packed chopped fresh cilantro

14 oz (398 mL) can kidney beans, rinsed and drained

In a non-stick skillet, cook the oil, onion, garlic and ginger on medium-low for 5 minutes. Add the chili, garam masala, paprika, turmeric and salt and cook for 2 minutes, stirring frequently. Add the chicken pieces and cook for 4 minutes, turning the chicken frequently. Add the tomatoes, cilantro and 1 cup (250 mL) of water and stir well.

Turn down the heat to a simmer, cover and cook for 15 minutes or until the chicken is cooked through. Add the kidney beans and cook for another 2 minutes.

Serve with rotis or rice. **SERVES 4**

A good lamb chop can knock off your socks, and I guarantee that this recipe is up for that task. Raita helps cool the heat from the spices and the dill in the rice balances all the flavours.

Lamb Chops with Raita and Dilled Brown Basmati Rice

Grilled Lamb Chops

2 Tbsp (30 mL) garam masala (see page 11)

1 Tbsp (15 mL) Italian seasoning

salt and pepper to taste

eight 6 oz (175 g) double-bone lamb chops

Raita

1 cup (250 mL) sour cream

½ cup (125 mL) buttermilk

juice and zest of 1 lemon

2 Tbsp (30 mL) chopped cilantro

pinch of garam masala (see page 11)

pinch of smoked paprika

salt and pepper to taste

Dilled Brown Basmati Rice

2 cups (500 mL) brown basmati rice

1 Tbsp (15 mL) dill

salt and pepper to taste

FOR THE LAMB CHOPS Combine the garam masala, Italian seasoning, salt and pepper and rub the mixture on the lamb chops.

Preheat the grill to medium-high. Gently place the chops on the grill and cook for 5 to 8 minutes per side, depending on how you like them. I prefer medium-rare, about 4 to 5 minutes per side. Let the chops sit for a few minutes before serving.

FOR THE RAITA In a large bowl, thoroughly combine the sour cream, buttermilk, lemon juice and zest, cilantro, garam masala, paprika, salt and pepper.

FOR THE RICE In a saucepan, bring the rice and seasonings to a boil in 4 cups (1 L) water. Turn down the heat to low, cover the saucepan and cook until the rice is done, about 45 minutes.

TO PLATE THE DISH Place a few spoonfuls of raita on each plate, topped with 2 lamb chops. Serve with the rice on the side. **SERVES 4**

Everyone loves this recipe, from the youngest kids to adults. Its playfulness and amazing flavours are perfect for any celebration. This is also a great recipe to work in some of your own favourite flavours. Have fun with it! Cooking with spices is easy and so delicious.

Lamb Tikkas with Mango and Mint Sauce

Lamb Tikka

1 lb (500 g) ground lamb

2 cups (500 mL) loosely packed chopped fresh fenugreek leaves

1 green chili, finely chopped

1 Tbsp (15 mL) grated ginger

1 Tbsp (15 mL) steak masala (see page 10)

1 tsp (5 mL) cardamom seeds

salt and pepper to taste

2 Tbsp (30 mL) crushed coriander seeds for coating

Mango and Mint Sauce

4 medium ripe mangoes, peeled and pitted

¼ cup (60 mL) loosely packed mint leaves

2 green onions, thinly sliced

1 green chili, minced

juice of ½ lemon

1 tsp (5 mL) ground cumin

pinch of salt and pepper

16 metal or bamboo skewers (see Note)

TO PREPARE THE LAMB TIKKA In a large bow,l mix the lamb, fenugreek leaves, chili, ginger, steak masala, cardamom seeds, salt and pepper.

Shape 2 spoonfuls of the mixture into a flattish ball, about 2 inches (5 cm) in diameter, and thread onto the end of a skewer. Sprinkle crushed coriander seeds over the ball to coat. Repeat with the remaining mixture and crushed coriander seeds.

Preheat the grill to medium-high and brush it with oil. Grill the lamb tikkas until cooked through, about 3 to 4 minutes per side.

TO PREPARE THE SAUCE Purée the mango, mint, green onions, chili, lemon juice, cumin, salt and pepper in a food processor until smooth but still slightly chunky.

In a saucepan, heat the sauce on low.

TO PLATE THE DISH Place a few tablespoons of the Mango and Mint Sauce in a shallow bowl. Gently place 4 lamb tikkas on the sauce. Serve with rice. **SERVES 4**

NOTE
If using bamboo skewers, soak them in water overnight.

Indian beer can be bought at most major liquor stores. Beer was introduced to India by the British, and a trip to India is not complete without tasting a good Indian beer. I prefer a light-tasting lager with plenty of malt, and it has to have a bite. It complements my spices perfectly, which is why I decided to add it to this marinade for ribs. If you can't find Indian beer, try any beer with a bite to it. The longer you barbecue the ribs, the more tender they become and the more intensely the flavours are infused.

BBQ Indian Beer Ribs

2 Tbsp (30 mL) smoked paprika

2 Tbsp (30 mL) fenugreek leaves

1 Tbsp (15 mL) dry mustard

1 Tbsp (15 mL) oregano

1 Tbsp (15 mL) garam masala (see page 11)

10 garlic cloves, finely diced

2-inch (5 cm) piece sugar cane

1 cup (250 mL) Indian lager

1 cup (250 mL) tomato paste

¼ cup (60 mL) honey

4 lb (1.8 kg) pork ribs

Thoroughly combine all the ingredients except the ribs to make a marinade. Place the ribs in a pan large enough to accommodate them in a single layer. Pour the marinade over the ribs, cover with plastic wrap and refrigerate for up to 3 hours.

Preheat the grill to medium-low. Wipe the excess marinade from the ribs and grill until the ribs are very tender, about 30 to 40 minutes.

Serve with Grated Cauliflower with Peas (page 62) and rice. **SERVES 4 TO 6**

A good relationship with your butcher goes a long way. In this recipe I prefer the ribs whole because it just looks prettier that way. At the butcher shop I go to, there is an older butcher who leaves the ribs whole for me, and tells me how to cook the recipe.

Indian-style Braised Short Ribs

¼ cup (60 mL) grapeseed oil

1 Tbsp (15 mL) coriander seeds

1 Tbsp (15 mL) cumin seeds

½ tsp (2 mL) red chili flakes

4 to 6 cardamom pods, cracked

¼ cup (60 mL) dried fenugreek leaves

3 lb (1.5 kg) beef short ribs, about 3 inches (8 cm) long

2 large onions, chopped

2 cups (500 mL) chopped celery

2 cups (500 mL) chopped carrots

3 Tbsp (45 mL) chopped garlic

4 cups (1 L) beef broth

bunch of fresh rosemary

several bay leaves

salt and pepper to taste

Preheat the oven to 325°F (160°C) degrees.

In a large, heavy-bottomed, ovenproof skillet, heat the oil on medium-high. Add the coriander seeds, cumin seeds, chili flakes, then the cardamom pods, then the fenugreek leaves. Add the short ribs. Brown the ribs on all sides, turning often to coat the ribs with oil and spices. Remove the ribs from the skillet and set aside.

Discard the excess fat and sauté the onions, celery, carrots and garlic for a few minutes, until softened. Add the ribs back to the skillet with the broth, rosemary, bay leaves, salt and pepper. Cover the skillet with a lid and bake for 2 hours or until the ribs almost fall off the bone.

Serve with Garlic and Coriander Broccoli (page 61) and rice. **SERVES 4**

When I ask for prime beef, my local butcher knows that it better have been dry-aged for at least 40 days. It is often difficult to find well-aged meat, but once you try it you will know exactly what I am talking about. Infused with the spices I chose for this recipe, this is a rare treat for your guests or just for you. I have cooked this several times just for myself and thoroughly enjoyed it with a nice glass of red wine.

Rib-eye Steak with Toasted Coriander Blue Cheese

¼ cup (60 mL) steak masala (see page 10)

four 6 oz (175 g) dry-aged rib-eye steak (I prefer 1½-inch/4 cm thick)

Toasted Coriander Blue Cheese

1 Tbsp (15 mL) coriander seeds

½ cup (125 mL) blue cheese

1 tsp (5 mL) smoked paprika

Sautéed Asparagus

1 Tbsp (5 mL) cooking oil

1 Tbsp (5 mL) chopped garlic

1 lb (500 g) asparagus, hard ends removed

salt and pepper to taste

Preheat the grill to medium-high. Sprinkle the steak masala on the steaks. Gently place the steaks on the heated grill and cook for about 3 to 5 minutes on each side for medium steaks, or to your preferred doneness. Let them sit for a few minutes before serving.

TO MAKE THE TOASTED CORIANDER BLUE CHEESE Toast the coriander seeds on low heat in a skillet for 30 seconds. Let them cool, then crush them with your hands. In a bowl, thoroughly combine the coriander seeds, blue cheese and paprika.

TO MAKE THE SAUTÉED ASPARAGUS In a saucepan, heat the oil on medium-high. Add the garlic and cook for 30 seconds. Add the asparagus and salt and pepper and cook, stirring frequently, until the asparagus is tender, about 10 to 12 minutes.

TO PLATE THE DISH Place the asparagus on a plate. Slice the cooked steaks and crumble Toasted Coriander Blue Cheese on top. **SERVES 4**

SUGGESTED WINE

2009 Merlot by CedarCreek Estate Winery

In India, my mother used to make vegetable sabji every day for lunch and even now, after 20 years, those aromas come to my mind when I think about stews. I decided to incorporate meat into a traditional Punjabi sabji, and I love how well the flavours came together.

Spiced Beef Sabji

2 Tbsp (30 mL) grapeseed oil

2 Tbsp (30 mL) flour

½ tsp (2 mL) ground cardamom

½ tsp (2 mL) salt

2 lb (1 kg) stewing beef, cubed

8 garlic cloves, crushed

1 Tbsp (15 mL) crushed coriander seeds

1 Tbsp (15 mL) ground cumin

¼ tsp (1 mL) ground cloves

⅓ cup (80 mL) tomato paste

3 large carrots, chopped into chunks

2 large potatoes, cubed

2 cups (500 mL) beef or vegetable broth

1 cup (250 mL) red wine

salt and pepper to taste

Heat the oil in a large non-stick skillet on medium-high. Combine the flour, ground cardamom and salt on a plate. Dip the beef cubes in the flour mixture, then cook them in the skillet, turning each cube until the meat is golden brown on all sides. Add the garlic, coriander seeds, cumin and cloves and cook for 10 seconds. Add the tomato paste and cook for 2 minutes, stirring well.

Transfer the meat mixture to a slow cooker. Add the carrots, potatoes, broth, wine, salt and pepper, and cook on high for 30 minutes. Turn down the heat to low and cook for 5 to 6 hours, until the meat is tender and the sauce is thickened.

Serve with rotis or rice. **SERVES 4**

Nothing beats a homemade giant burger. You can cater to every palate by adding the ingredients you like. I like to add green chilies for a nice heat, but Anoop likes her food mild. This recipe is for mild palates and you will love the great flavours of the spices.

Anoop's Giant Beef and Paneer Burger

1 egg

¼ cup (60 mL) dried breadcrumbs

1 small onion, finely chopped

2 tsp (10 mL) brown mustard seeds

½ tsp (2 mL) cumin seeds

¼ tsp (1 mL) cardamom seeds

¼ cup (60 mL) loosely packed fresh curry leaves

salt and pepper to taste

1 lb (500 g) lean ground beef

½ cup (125 mL) coarsely grated paneer (see page 51)

4 hamburger buns

Preheat the grill to medium. In a large bowl, beat the egg, then stir in the breadcrumbs, onion, mustard seeds, cumin seeds, cardamom seeds, curry leaves, salt and pepper. Add the ground beef and paneer and mix until just combined.

Divide into quarters and shape into 4 patties. Grill the patties with the lid closed for 12 to 14 minutes, flipping once, until they are cooked through.

Serve in buns with lettuce, tomatoes, onions and pickles. **SERVES 4**

For weekend lunches or dinners, Aaron often requests these burgers and enjoys them with my homemade chutney.

Paneer and Beef Burger

1 lb (500 g) minced beef

½ lb (250 g) coarsely grated paneer (see page 51)

½ cup (125 mL) dried breadcrumbs

¼ cup (60 mL) finely chopped ripe mango

1 Tbsp (15 mL) grated ginger

1 Tbsp (15 mL) fennel seeds

1 Tbsp (15 mL) ground cumin

1 Tbsp (15 mL) ground coriander

1 tsp (5 mL) smoked paprika

salt to taste

Preheat the grill to medium-high.

In a large bowl, stir together all the ingredients until evenly combined. Form the mixture into 2-inch (5 cm) patties. Reduce the grill to medium and gently place the patties on the grill. Cook for about 9 to 12 minutes until cooked through, turning frequently to make sure both sides are browned.

Serve in buns with lettuce, tomatoes and onions, and your favourite sauce or chutney. **SERVES 4**

I prefer bison meat to beef as it has more flavour and is extra lean. What I love about this recipe is that everything goes in one bowl and it's ready. All you have to do is grill to perfection and enjoy!

Bison Burgers

2 lb (1 kg) ground bison meat

2 eggs

1½ cups (375 mL) dried breadcrumbs

1 medium red onion, finely chopped

¼ cup (60 mL) loosely packed fresh curry leaves

¼ cup (60 mL) fenugreek leaves

1 Tbsp (15 mL) finely chopped ginger

1 Tbsp (15 mL) garam masala (see page 11)

1 Tbsp (15 mL) coriander seeds

Mix everything together in a large bowl. Shape into 4 to 6 patties, depending on how large you like them. Preheat the grill to medium-high and grill the burgers for about 5 minutes per side, until they are browned on both sides and cooked through.

Serve in buns with your favourite burger toppings.

SERVES 4 TO 6

Indian-style Thanksgiving

I would like to share the recipes that I use for Thanksgiving dinner in my kitchen. Every dish I make is full of love and infused with the great aromas of my spices. My family and friends can never get enough of these dishes and there are never any leftovers for lunches the next day. After trying my recipes, you will never go back to eating a traditional salt-and-pepper-based turkey meal. You will want to add a few of my spices to give a kick to the old-fashioned traditions.

The recipes in this section will feed a family of 6 to 8 people.

The Fabulous Spiced Turkey

14 lb (6.5 kg) turkey

1 Tbsp (15 mL) garam masala
(see page 11)

3 Tbsp (45 mL) mild curry
masala (see page 12)

½ tsp (2 mL) salt

½ tsp (2 mL) pepper

juice of 1 lemon

2 Granny Smith apples, peeled,
cored and sliced

1 garlic bulb, cloves separated
and peeled

handful of cilantro leaves

¼ cup (60 mL) dried fenugreek
leaves

1 Tbsp (15 mL) ground cardamom

1 Tbsp (15 mL) smoked paprika

1 tsp (5 mL) ground turmeric

½ tsp (2 mL) ground cinnamon

red grapes and herbs for garnish

Preheat the oven to 400°F (200°C).

Wash the turkey thoroughly with cold water and pat dry with paper towels. Lay it on a clean cutting board and season the skin and cavity with 1 Tbsp (15 mL) of the garam masala, the mild curry masala, salt, pepper and lemon juice. Stuff the apples, garlic and cilantro into the cavity, then tie the legs together with kitchen twine and tuck the wings behind the back of the turkey.

Mix together the remaining 2 Tbsp (30 mL) garam masala, the fenugreek leaves, cardamom, paprika, turmeric and cinnamon in a small bowl. Loosen the skin on the breast of the turkey and rub some of the spice mixture under it, taking care not to tear the skin, then rub the remaining mixture liberally over the rest of the turkey.

Place the turkey in a large roasting pan and cover it with aluminum foil. Bake for 1 to 1½ hours at 400°F (200°C). Turn the oven down to 325°F (160°C) and continue cooking until the turkey is cooked through and the juices run clear, another 4 to 6 hours.

Place on a serving platter and garnish with red grapes and herbs. Allow to rest for 15 minutes before carving.

SUGGESTED WINE
2009 Merlot by Poplar Grove Winery

Masala Mashed Potatoes

6 potatoes, peeled and cubed

6 garlic cloves, peeled

1 cup (250 mL) milk

¼ cup (60 mL) unsalted butter

1 Tbsp (15 mL) cumin seeds, toasted

1 tsp (5 mL) smoked paprika

salt and pepper to taste

In a large saucepan, cover the potatoes and garlic with water. Bring to a boil, turn the heat down and simmer until the potatoes are cooked through, about 8 to 10 minutes. Drain the potatoes. Add the milk, butter, cumin seeds, paprika, salt and pepper and mash the potatoes until smooth.

Cranberry Sauce with Cloves

In a saucepan, heat the cranberry juice, orange juice, lemon juice and zest, sugar, paprika and cloves on medium-high until the mixture boils. Add the cranberries and turn the heat to medium-low. Cook until the cranberries start softening, about 10 to 12 minutes. Remove from the heat and let cool.

1 cup (250 mL) cranberry juice

¼ cup (60 mL) orange juice

juice and zest of 1 lemon

¾ cup (185 mL) sugar

½ tsp (2 mL) smoked paprika

¼ tsp (1 mL) ground cloves

10 oz (300 g) cranberries

Pickled Onions

1 cup (250 mL) red wine vinegar

½ cup (125 mL) sugar

10 pearl onions, quartered

8 green cardamom pods

6 whole star anise

1 Tbsp (15 mL) coriander seeds, toasted

In a small pot, bring the vinegar to a boil, add the sugar and stir to dissolve. Add the rest of the ingredients, boil for 1 minute and turn off the heat.

Once the onions have cooled, put them in a jar with their liquid and refrigerate for up to 1 week.

Brussels Sprouts with Coriander Seeds

In a skillet, cook the oil and garlic on medium-high until the garlic is golden brown, about 20 seconds. Add the coriander seeds, chili flakes, salt and pepper and cook for 10 seconds. Add the Brussels sprouts and ¼ cup (60 mL) of water. Turn the heat to low. Cook until the sprouts are tender and fully coated with spices, about 10 to 12 minutes.

2 Tbsp (30 mL) grapeseed oil

1 Tbsp (15 mL) chopped garlic

1 Tbsp (15 mL) coriander seeds, crushed

½ tsp (2 mL) red chili flakes

salt and pepper to taste

1 lb (500 g) brussels sprouts, halved

rice & breads

After Anoop tried the yellow sweet rice at the temple for the first time, she came home and asked me why I never made that rice for her. That was my inspiration to create this recipe.

Anoop's Yellow Rice

3 Tbsp (45 mL) butter

8 whole cloves

8 cardamom pods

few drops of yellow food colouring

1 cup (250 mL) basmati rice

½ cup (125 mL) cashews

¾ cup (185 mL) sugar

In a saucepan, stir the butter, cloves, cardamom pods and food colouring with the rice and cashews. Cook on medium heat for 1 minute. Add 2 cups (500 mL) water and bring to a boil. Turn the heat to low, cover and cook until the rice is done, about 20 minutes. Turn off the heat and stir in the sugar.

Put a tea towel over the saucepan and let it sit for 10 minutes. Remove the cardamom pods and cloves before serving. **SERVES 4**

Saffron is more expensive than gold, so I use it wisely. A few strands of good saffron go far, and when you add it to spiced cashews with basmati rice, you know it's being used for a good cause.

There's never plain rice in my kitchen. It always has to be cooked with peas and the warm, earthy flavour of cumin. Trust me, after eating this, you will never want to eat simple steamed rice again.

My Everyday Rice

2 Tbsp (30 mL) grapeseed oil

1 medium onion, chopped

1 medium potato, peeled and diced

1 cup (250 mL) frozen peas

½ cup (125 mL) cashews

1 Tbsp (15 mL) cumin seeds

salt and pepper to taste

1 cup (250 mL) basmati rice

few threads of saffron

In a saucepan, combine the oil, onion, potato, peas, cashews, cumin seeds, salt and pepper, and cook for 4 minutes. Add the rice, saffron and 2 cups (500 mL) water and bring to a boil. Turn down the heat to low, cover and cook until the rice is done, about 20 minutes. Turn off the heat, put a tea towel over the saucepan and let it sit for 10 minutes before serving. **SERVES 4**

I went to Paris two years in a row, the first time as a tourist and the second time to enjoy and learn about French flavours. After eating a traditional risotto there, I knew I had to try it with some flavours that we use in South India. After eating this, I knew I could never go back to eating simple risotto again.

Indian-inspired Risotto

4 cups (1 L) vegetable stock

4 Tbsp (60 mL) butter

1 small onion, finely chopped

5 whole star anise

12 green cardamom pods

1 Tbsp (15 mL) mild curry masala (see page 12)

1 tsp (5 mL) brown mustard seeds

¼ cup (60 mL) loosely packed fresh curry leaves

2 cups (500 mL) thinly sliced mushrooms (combination of oyster, shiitake and portobello)

1 cup (250 mL) arborio rice

½ cup (125 mL) dry white wine

½ cup (125 mL) shaved Parmesan

½ tsp (2 mL) red chili flakes

Bring the stock to a simmer over medium heat. Turn the heat to low and keep the stock hot.

Melt 2 Tbsp (30 mL) of the butter in a large saucepan over medium heat. When it begins to foam, add the onion and cook until soft, about 3 minutes. Add the spices and curry leaves and continue to cook for 1 minute. Stir in the mushrooms and cook until they begin to caramelize, about 5 minutes.

Turn the heat to low. Add the rice, stirring so it is well coated with butter, then add the wine, stirring constantly as it is absorbed into the rice. Add the hot stock ¼ cup (60 mL) at a time, continuing to stir constantly. Once each addition of stock is absorbed into the rice, add another portion. The rice is done when it is tender and creamy in consistency, about 30 minutes. Remove it from the heat, stir in the remaining 2 Tbsp (30 mL) butter and season with salt to taste.

To serve, spoon into wide, shallow bowls, removing the cardamom pods and star anise. Garnish with shaved cheese and a scattering of red chili flakes. **SERVES 6 TO 8**

SUGGESTED WINE

2010 Syrah by Nichol Vineyard & Estate Winery

Anoop has no interest in learning how to make rotis but she loves to eat them. Aaron, on the other hand, grabs his own rolling pin and starts making them. I use whole wheat flour because it is healthy. These rotis make a perfect shell for lunch wraps. They freeze very well, but be sure to put parchment paper between them so they don't stick together in the freezer.

Simply Perfect Roti

2 cups (500 mL) whole wheat flour

1 tsp (5 mL) ground cumin

1 tsp (5 mL) ground coriander

pinch of salt

½–1 cup (125–250 mL) water

flaxseed oil for brushing

Combine the flour, cumin, coriander, salt and ½ cup (125 mL) water in a large bowl and mix by hand until it begins to form a ball. If there is excess flour and it seems dry, add more water gradually, until the mixture is a dough. Knead until it has a smooth consistency, like pizza dough. The dough should be soft and smooth.

Divide the dough into 6 equal-sized balls. Flatten one ball into a disc, then roll it out on a floured surface into a very thin circle approximately 6 inches (15 cm) in diameter, like a tortilla.

Heat a non-stick pan on medium-low. Gently place the roti in the pan and cook for 1 minute, until the dough begins to bubble and turn brown. Flip the roti and continue to cook until it's golden and crispy, about 1 minute. Remove from the pan and brush with the oil to keep it moist.

Repeat the process with the remaining dough balls.

Serve with your favourite sauce, curry or stew. **MAKES 6 ROTIS**

I received emails from all over North America when my show Spice Goddess *was launched. People were so glad to find that it included so many gluten-free recipes. I received several requests to make a gluten-free roti, so I created this recipe using chickpea flour. They have a very soft texture and are absolutely to die for.*

Chickpea Fenugreek Roti

2 cups (500 mL) chickpea flour

1 cup (250 mL) loosely packed finely chopped fresh fenugreek leaves

1 Tbsp (15 mL) garam masala (see page 11)

pinch of salt

½–1 cup (125–250 mL) water

flaxseed oil for brushing

Combine the flour, fenugreek leaves, garam masala, salt and ½ cup (125 mL) of the water in a large bowl by hand until it begins to form a ball. If there is excess flour and it seems dry, add more water gradually, until the mixture is a dough. Knead until it has a smooth consistency, like pizza dough. The dough should be soft and smooth.

Divide the dough into 6 equal-sized balls. Flatten one ball into a disc, then and roll it out on a floured surface into a very thin circle approximately 6 inches (15 cm) in diameter, like a tortilla.

Heat a non-stick pan on medium-low. Gently place the roti in the pan and cook for 1 minute, until the dough begins to bubble and turn brown. Flip the roti and continue to cook until it's golden and crispy, about 1 minute. Remove from the pan and brush with the oil to keep it moist.

Repeat the process with the remaining dough balls.

Serve with your favourite sauce, curry or stew. **MAKES 6 ROTIS**

Kids often want pancakes or waffles on the weekends, but my daughter, Anoop, asks for these potato parathas. A simple roti in my village is a flat bread like a tortilla, but as soon as you add any filling, we call it paratha. This is one of her favourite recipes, and she has even got her friends hooked. Serve them with fresh homemade yogurt and you too might not want pancakes for breakfast.

Potato Parathas

1 cup (250 mL) mashed potatoes

1 small green chili, minced (keep the seeds if you like the heat)

¼ cup (60 mL) chopped cilantro

2 Tbsp (30 mL) grated ginger

1 Tbsp (15 mL) ground coriander

1 tsp (5 mL) salt

1 recipe Plain Roti Dough (see sidebar)

In a bowl, thoroughly mix the potato, chili, cilantro, ginger, coriander and salt.

Take a golf ball–sized piece of roti dough and shape it into a round disc. Roll out the disc on a floured surface until it is a very thin circle like a tortilla.

Place 2 spoonfuls of filling on the centre of the roti. Roll out a second roti and place it over the filling. Press the rotis together and gently roll over them a few times with the rolling pin.

Heat a large non-stick skillet on medium heat. Gently place the paratha in the skillet and cook for 1 or 2 minutes, until small bubbly spots appear, then flip it over to cook the second side, about 1 or 2 minutes. Remove from the pan and keep warm.

Repeat this process with the remaining dough and filling. **MAKES 4 PARATHAS**

Plain Roti Dough

2 cups (500 mL) whole wheat flour   *¾–1 cup (185–250 mL) water*

Combine the flour and water in a bowl and knead until it forms a smooth, round ball similar to stiff pizza dough.

Coconut Chicken Paratha

2 Tbsp (30 mL) grapeseed oil, plus ¼ cup (60 mL) for brushing

1 small red onion, chopped

2 Tbsp (30 mL) chopped garlic

1 Tbsp (15 mL) chopped ginger

1 Tbsp (15 mL) cumin seeds

1 Tbsp (15 mL) garam masala (see page 11)

1 tsp (5 mL) red chili flakes

1 tsp (5 mL) ground turmeric

salt and pepper

1 lb (500 g) ground chicken

14 oz (398 mL) can coconut milk

3 cups (750 mL) whole wheat flour

In a skillet, cook the oil, onion, garlic and ginger on medium-high for 2 minutes. Add the cumin seeds, garam masala, chili flakes, turmeric, salt and pepper and cook for 30 seconds. Add the chicken and cook for 5 minutes, stirring frequently. Add the coconut milk and cook until the chicken is cooked through, about 10 to 12 minutes.

In a bowl, combine the flour and 1 cup (250 mL) of the chicken filling. Knead until the dough has a soft, smooth consistency like pizza dough. Divide it into 6 equal-sized balls. Flatten one ball into a disc, then roll it out on a floured surface into a thin circle approximately 6 inches (15 cm) in diameter, like a tortilla.

Heat a non-stick pan on medium-low. Gently place the paratha in the pan and cook for 1 to 2 minutes, until the dough begins to bubble and turn brown. Flip the paratha and continue to cook it until it's golden and crispy, about 1 to 2 minutes. Remove from the pan and brush with a little oil to keep it moist.

Repeat the process with the remaining dough balls.

Enjoy the paratha on its own or serve with the remaining chicken filling. Any leftover chicken filling can be stored in the fridge for up to 2 days. **MAKES 6 PARATHAS**

desserts

This is a refreshing, healthy and light dessert that you can prepare right before your guests arrive. What I love about this is that you can serve it with any seasonal fruit, nuts, granola or peanut brittle.

Cardamom Yogurt with Toasted Coconut Flakes

2 cups (500 mL) plain yogurt

1 tsp (5 mL) saffron threads

½ tsp (2 mL) ground cardamom

2 Tbsp (30 mL) crushed pistachios

2 Tbsp (30 mL) maple syrup

¼ cup (60 mL) toasted coconut flakes for garnish

2 cups (500 mL) fresh mixed berries for garnish

Line a large sieve with cheesecloth, set it over a bowl and pour in the yogurt. Fold the edges of the cheesecloth over the yogurt so it is completely covered. Refrigerate the sieve and bowl for 12 hours or overnight.

In a small bowl, pour about 2 Tbsp (30 mL) boiling water over the saffron threads. Let steep for 5 minutes, then strain, reserving the saffron.

In a large bowl, combine the drained yogurt, steeped saffron and cardamom with the pistachios and maple syrup and mix well. Pour into individual bowls and refrigerate.

Sprinkle with toasted coconut flakes and fresh berries just before serving. **SERVES 4**

This was the very first dessert I had when I came to Canada. I loved the flavours, but something was missing. I use thawed frozen bananas because the fresh ones take a long time to soften to a smooth texture. It's also a great way to use up old bananas. After I created this recipe, my family and friends were all pleased. Here it is, for everyone who dares to take the banana split challenge. I bet you can't have it only one time!

Banana Split

¼ cup (60 mL) butter

2 Tbsp (30 mL) brown sugar

8 brown cardamom pods

1 Tbsp (15 mL) fennel seeds

three 2-inch (5 cm) cinnamon sticks

2 frozen bananas, thawed, peeled and cut in half lengthwise

2 cups (500 mL) vanilla ice cream

1 cup (250 mL) fresh raspberries

1 cup (250 mL) broken peanut brittle

In a skillet, cook the butter with the sugar, spices and bananas on low heat for 30 minutes, turning the bananas after 15 minutes.

Gently lift the bananas out with a spatula and arrange them on a plate. Add a scoop or two of ice cream on the side. Sprinkle with raspberries and peanut brittle.

SERVES 4

Kulfi is ice cream. Once when I was in grade 4, I sold my math book to the kulfi vendor for just one scoop. I paid the price when I went to school the next day, but it was worth it.

Mango Kulfi (Indian Ice Cream)

2 cups (500 mL) mango juice

1 cup (250 mL) ripe mango chunks

1 banana

2 cups (500 mL) plain or vanilla frozen yogurt

1 Tbsp (15 mL) lemon juice

½ tsp (2 mL) ground cardamom

½ tsp (2 mL) fennel seeds

½ cup (125 mL) diced mango for garnish (optional)

½ cup (125 mL) chopped pistachios for garnish (optional)

In a food processor, blend the mango juice, mango chunks and banana until smooth. Add the frozen yogurt and lemon juice and process until well combined. Add the cardamom and fennel seeds and blend well.

Transfer the mixture to the frozen insert of a commercial ice-cream maker and churn according to the manufacturer's instructions. Alternatively, spoon the mixture into a large glass baking dish, cover and freeze for 2 to 3 hours, until frozen. If you want soft ice cream, stir it every hour while it is freezing.

Serve in a bowl, garnished with diced mango and pistachios. **SERVES 6 TO 8**

Ginger and chocolate ice cream. Yes! How come I never thought of this idea before? The curry flavour from the turmeric and spiciness from the ginger combined with the sweetness from the chocolate make this dessert absolutely mouth-watering. I usually try not to use whipping cream in my recipes, but since this is a dessert it is a rare treat. Everything in moderation, I say.

Ginger and White Chocolate Ice Cream

2 cups (500 mL) whipping cream

1 cup (250 mL) whole milk

1 Tbsp (15 mL) ground ginger

½ tsp (2 mL) ground turmeric

½ tsp (2 mL) smoked paprika

¼ tsp (1 mL) salt

6 egg yolks

1 cup (250 mL) sugar

¼ cup (60 mL) white chocolate chips

In a medium-sized pot on high heat, bring the whipping cream, milk, ginger, turmeric, paprika and salt to a boil. Turn off the heat, cover with a lid and let sit for the flavours to infuse for 10 minutes.

In a large bowl, whisk the egg yolks and sugar together until pale and thick. Slowly add the hot cream mixture while whisking constantly to temper the eggs. If the cream is added too quickly, the eggs will scramble.

Pour the mixture back into the pot and cook over low heat, stirring constantly, until it is thick enough to coat the back of a spoon, about 10 to 12 minutes.

Pour into a clean bowl and refrigerate for 2 hours, or until well chilled.

Stir in the chocolate chips and freeze in an ice-cream maker, following the manufacturer's instructions. Alternatively, spoon the mixture into a large glass baking dish, cover and freeze for 2 to 3 hours, until frozen. If you want soft ice cream, stir it every hour while it is freezing.

SERVES 6 TO 8

When I would get sick in India, my mom would make me this dessert to cheer me up. Sometimes I wanted to be sick just so I could eat this special treat. The great thing about being old now is that I can make this whenever I feel like it—even if it's a few times a week.

Toasted Brioche in Spiced Milk

2 cups (500 mL) 2% milk

6 whole star anise

8 green cardamom pods

10 whole cloves

two 3-inch (8 cm) cinnamon sticks

2 Tbsp (30 mL) sugar

1-inch (2.5 cm) piece ginger

3 Tbsp (45 mL) butter

4 thick slices brioche or challah bread

fresh berries for garnish

 pinch of ground cinnamon

In a saucepan on medium-high, bring the milk, spices, sugar and ginger to a boil. Turn down the heat to low and simmer for 10 minutes to infuse the milk with the spices. Keep warm.

Melt the butter in a non-stick skillet on medium heat. When it begins to foam, brown the bread slices in the skillet for 2 minutes on each side.

In 4 shallow bowls, add ½ cup of the milk and spice mixture, making sure that each bowl has an assortment of the whole spices. Gently top with a slice of the toasted bread. Garnish with berries and a sprinkle of cinnamon.

SERVES 4

My mom's rice pudding was famous among the entire village. It was a rare treat because she only made it once in a while. She would sit by the barbecue pit and all her friends would sit around her. They would sip chai and gossip while my mom slowly stirred the milk that turned into this irresistible dessert.

Mom's Rice Pudding

8 cups (2 L) whole milk

1 cup (250 mL) short-grain white rice

¼ cup (60 mL) slivered almonds

¼ cup (60 mL) raisins

¼ cup (60 mL) sugar

12 cardamom pods

10 whole cloves

In a large saucepan on high heat, bring all the ingredients to a boil. Turn down the heat to low and simmer, uncovered, for 45 minutes, stirring occasionally, until the milk is absorbed and the mixture has thickened to resemble risotto.

Remove the cardamom pods and cloves before serving. Serve hot or cold and top with seasonal fruit such as mango or berries. **SERVES 4 TO 6**

Gajar means carrots in Punjabi. This dessert is similar to carrot cake, but with an Indian twist. We serve this at weddings or big festivals like Diwali. In the early morning of Diwali, my father would send my brother to the bakery for boxes filled with gajrela to give as gifts to friends and family members. I use organic carrots as they add more sweetness. The floral flavours from the cardamom combined with the nuttiness from the pistachios make this dessert irresistible.

Gajrela (Carrot Dessert)

1 lb (500 g) carrots, peeled and grated (organic are best)

2 cups (500 mL) whole milk

½ cup (125 mL) ricotta cheese

¼ cup (60 mL) cranberries

3 Tbsp (45 mL) honey

2 Tbsp (30 mL) chopped toasted almonds

1 tsp (5 mL) ground cardamom

¼ tsp (1 mL) ground cloves

¼ tsp (1 mL) ground nutmeg

In a large saucepan, combine all the ingredients and bring to a boil over medium heat. Turn down the heat to low and simmer, stirring occasionally, until the carrots are soft and the mixture has thickened, about 15 to 18 minutes.

Serve warm. **SERVES 4**

No Indian wedding is complete unless the guests are served gulab jamun. These are tiny, deep-fried, round mini donuts, very sweet and very addicting. Since they are deep-fried, they are a special treat in my kitchen as I make them only for Diwali, the Indian festival that occurs in the fall.

Gulab Jamun (Indian Mini Donuts)

Syrup

5 cups (1.25 L) sugar

4 cups (1 L) water

10 green cardamom pods

6 brown cardamom pods

10 whole cloves

6 whole star anise

two 3-inch (8 cm) cinnamon sticks

Gulab Jamun

3 cups (750 mL) powdered milk

1 cup (250 mL) all-purpose flour

1 tsp (5 mL) ground fennel

½ tsp (2 mL) baking soda

1¾ cups (435 mL) 35% whipping cream

½ cup (125 mL) grapeseed oil

¼ cup (60 mL) finely grated coconut flakes

FOR THE SYRUP In a medium saucepan on high heat, bring the sugar, water, cardamom, cloves, star anise and cinnamon to a boil. Turn down the heat to low and simmer until the sugar has dissolved and the syrup is slightly thickened, about 25 minutes. Let cool slightly.

FOR THE GULAB JAMUN Combine the powdered milk, flour, fennel and baking soda. Slowly stir in the whipping cream until a loose dough forms.

Oil your hands and shape the dough into balls about the size of golf balls.

In a high-sided frying pan, heat the cooking oil over very low heat and carefully begin to add the dough balls. Fry them slowly, turning gently, until they are golden on all sides, 2 to 3 minutes per doughnut. Be careful not to burn them.

Remove the gulab jamun as they are cooked and immerse them in the syrup. Let them sit in the syrup for at least 15 minutes.

Remove the gulab jamun from the syrup and serve warm or at room temperature. Sprinkle with coconut flakes before serving. **MAKES 14 TO 16 GULAB JAMUN**

GULAB JAMUN (INDIAN MINI DONUTS)
AND SPICED MANGO CRÈME BRÛLÉE
(PAGE 160)

Besan (Indian Fudge)

2 cups (500 mL) sugar

1 cup (250 mL) water

1 tsp (5 mL) fennel seeds

1 tsp (5 mL) ground cardamom

¼ tsp (1 mL) ground cinnamon

⅛ tsp (0.5 mL) ground cloves

pinch of saffron

¾ cup (185 mL) butter

2 cups (500 mL) chickpea flour

Butter an 8-inch (20 cm) square baking pan.

In a saucepan set on high heat, bring the sugar, water, fennel seeds, cardamom, cinnamon, cloves and saffron to a boil. Turn down the heat and simmer until the syrup is thick enough to form a thread when pinched between thumb and forefinger, about 15 minutes. (To test, put a little syrup on a saucer and let it cool slightly before pinching.) Remove from the heat.

In a large skillet on medium-low, melt the butter. Add the chickpea flour and cook, stirring constantly, until it turns a deep golden brown, about 8 minutes.

Stir the butter-flour mixture into the syrup, then press the mixture into the baking pan and let it set, uncovered, at room temperature for about 1 hour.

Cut into squares and serve. **MAKES 16 TO 20 SQUARES**

My kids' favourite part of this recipe is licking the spoon. I love the chewiness of the cookies after they are baked. Ginger gives a nice heat to the cookies that balances the sweetness of the chocolate. A bit of licorice flavour from the fennel adds uniqueness to the recipe.

Ginger Fennel Chocolate Chip Cookies

1½ cups (375 mL) all-purpose flour

1 tsp (5 mL) baking powder

1 Tbsp (15 mL) ground ginger

1 tsp (5 mL) ground fennel

1 tsp (5 mL) fennel seeds

¼ tsp (1 mL) salt

½ cup (125 mL) soft unsalted butter

¾ cup (185 mL) brown sugar

1 Tbsp (15 mL) corn syrup

1 tsp (5 mL) grated ginger

1 egg

1 tsp (5 mL) vanilla extract

1 cup (250 mL) chocolate chips

Preheat the oven to 375°F (190°C).

In a bowl, thoroughly mix the flour, baking powder, ginger, ground fennel, fennel seeds and salt.

In a deep bowl, cream together the butter and sugar. Add the corn syrup, ginger, egg and vanilla extract and mix very well. Add the flour mixture slowly, in two batches, and mix well. Stir in the chocolate chips.

Grease a cookie sheet. Scoop spoonfuls of dough onto the cookie sheet. Bake until the cookies are golden brown, about 12 to 15 minutes.

Serve warm with a glass of milk. **MAKES 14 TO 16 COOKIES**

When my girlfriends come for dinner at my place, these are always on the menu. Last time when I did not bake them because I had just returned from a business trip, my girlfriends went straight to my kitchen and started making them. According to them, if they don't eat these at my dinners, the meal is not complete. After you try these, you will know exactly what they are talking about.

My Favourite Brownies

8 oz (250 g) dark chocolate chips

8 oz (250 g) semi-sweet chocolate chips

10 oz (300 g) butter

6 eggs

1 cup (250 mL) sugar

1 Tbsp (10 mL) ground cardamom

1 tsp (5 mL) ground fennel

½ tsp (2 mL) salt

1½ cups (375 mL) all-purpose flour

Preheat the oven to 325°F (160°C). Grease and flour a 9- × 13-inch (3.5-L) baking pan.

Melt the chocolate chips and butter in the top of a double boiler over low heat. Let cool slightly.

Beat the eggs and sugar together until thick and pale yellow in colour. Add the cooled chocolate mixture and stir well to combine. Sift in the cardamom, fennel and salt along with the flour, and stir until completely combined.

Pour into the prepared pan. Bake for 30 minutes, or until an inserted toothpick comes out clean. Let cool and cut into squares. Serve with ice cream. **MAKES 18 TO 20 SQUARES**

Aaron always wants to make this dessert, and he does not even ask me for it anymore. He quietly starts peeling apples and puts the toppings together. He heats the oven and when the oven reaches the temperature and beeps, I hear the sound and know that my boy is up to no good, or to something very good. This recipe is dedicated to my little baker.

Aaron's Apple Crisp

Topping

½ cup (125 mL) all-purpose flour

½ cup (125 mL) rolled oats

½ cup (125 mL) brown sugar

¼ cup (60 mL) unsalted butter

2 Tbsp (30 mL) pumpkin seeds

½ tsp (2 mL) ground cardamom

½ tsp (2 mL) cinnamon

¼ tsp (1 mL) ground nutmeg

⅛ tsp (0.5 mL) salt

Filling

5 Granny Smith apples, peeled, cored and thinly sliced

¼ cup (60 mL) sugar

¼ cup (60 mL) water

zest of 1 lemon

Preheat the oven to 325°F (160°C).

TO PREPARE THE TOPPING In a bowl, thoroughly mix the flour, oats, sugar, butter, pumpkin seeds, cardamom, cinnamon, nutmeg and salt.

TO PREPARE THE FILLING In an 8- × 4-inch (1.5 L) loaf pan, layer the apples and cover them with the sugar, water and lemon zest and then the topping mixture.

Bake for 30 minutes, until the topping is crispy.

Serve warm with your favourite ice cream. **SERVES 4**

I was in Paris two years in a row. After eating crème brûlée in different cafés and restaurants, I knew I would have to try making it with my sweet spices. I came home and tried the dish with mango because it's my favourite fruit, and it goes well with the licorice flavours of fennel. After eating this, I can never go back to eating the regular crème brûlées. I am sure you will feel the same after trying this.

Spiced Mango Crème Brûlée

2 cups (500 mL) milk

1 Tbsp (15 mL) sugar

1 tsp (5 mL) ground fennel

½ tsp (2 mL) ground cardamom

¼ tsp (1 mL) ground cloves

4 medium-sized ripe mangoes, peeled, pitted and finely chopped

4 egg yolks

5 Tbsp (75 mL) sugar

Preheat the oven to 300°F (150°C).

In a medium saucepan, combine the milk, sugar, fennel, cardamom, cloves and mango. Bring to a boil on medium-high, then remove from the heat and cover with a tight-fitting lid. Let the flavours infuse for 15 to 20 minutes. Let the mixture cool and use a hand blender to blend thoroughly.

In a bowl, beat the egg yolks and 1 Tbsp (15 mL) of the sugar until thick and pale. Slowly pour the milk-mango mixture into the beaten egg yolks, whisking constantly to prevent the eggs from scrambling.

Pour the mixture back into the saucepan and cook over low heat for 3 to 5 minutes, until it is thick enough to coat the back of a spoon.

Pour into 4 shallow crème brûlée dishes or ramekins, place in a baking pan large enough to accommodate them, and pour water into the pan to come halfway up the dishes. Bake until set but still slightly jiggly, about 30 minutes. If they aren't done after 30 minutes, check every 5 minutes until they are set. Remove from the water bath and let cool for 15 to 20 minutes on the counter. Place in the refrigerator to finish cooling for about 1 hour.

Sprinkle 1 Tbsp (15 mL) sugar evenly on top of each crème brûlée. Melt the sugar with a blowtorch, or place the ramekins under the broiler until it has caramelized, about 3 to 5 minutes. Serve immediately. **SERVES 4**

SUGGESTED WINE

2011 Crab Apple by Elephant Island Orchard Wines

drinks

When Anoop was eight years old, she had a lemonade stand because she wanted to buy her very first Barbie. Until then, all her toys were bought from garage sales as we could not afford to buy brand-new toys. After selling this lemonade, she was able to buy a Barbie as well as a summer tent for herself. I enjoy the herbs and spices in the drink, but if you'd like, strain them before drinking.

Spiced Lemonade

1 whole star anise

1 tsp (5 mL) fennel seeds

½ tsp (2 mL) cardamom seeds

1 cup (250 mL) ice

2 Tbsp (30 mL) sugar

1 tsp (5 mL) grated ginger

juice of 2 lemons

zest of 1 lemon

handful of fresh mint leaves for garnish

In a small skillet on low heat, toast the star anise, fennel seeds and cardamom seeds for 15 seconds. Grind them to a powder in a spice grinder.

In a blender, pulse all the ingredients, including the spice powder, with 2 cups (500 mL) water until the ice is crushed.

Serve cold. **SERVES 2**

Lassi is a cooling drink that is often served during hot summer days. A traditional lassi is made with plain yogurt, ice, salt and pepper. My sweet tooth inspired me to create this recipe that can be served as a refreshing drink or as a dessert. When my girlfriends are visiting, I sometimes add a shot of vodka to give a little kick to the lassi. I add rosewater to give a floral flavour. You can find it in any specialty grocery store.

Mango Lassi

1 cup (250 mL) low-fat plain yogurt

1 cup (250 mL) mango pulp (or fresh mango chunks)

½ cup (125 mL) crushed ice

¼ tsp (1 mL) rosewater

¼ tsp (1 mL) ground cardamom

¼ tsp (1 mL) ground cloves

Purée all the ingredients in a blender with 1 cup (250 mL) water until very smooth. Serve immediately. **SERVES 2**

Chocolate shakes and vanilla shakes are very good, but wait until you try my papaya shake. Yogurt makes it healthy, and the naturally sweet papaya flavour makes this dessert guilt-free. You can ask for seconds without worrying about your diet.

Papaya Shake

3 medium extra-ripe papayas, peeled and seeds removed

2 cups (500 mL) low-fat plain yogurt

2 cups (500 mL) ice cubes

2 Tbsp (30 mL) sugar

2 Tbsp (30 mL) finely chopped mint

½ tsp (2 mL) ground cloves

½ tsp (2 mL) ground cardamom

Blend all the ingredients in a blender until smooth and creamy. Serve immediately. **SERVES 4**

When my girlfriends visit, I serve them champagne every time because I want to celebrate how blessed I am to have them in my life. Lately, I started serving champagne with a twist, and everyone asks for seconds.

Spiced Bubbly

In a martini shaker, thoroughly mix the orange juice, lemon juice and zest, cardamom and paprika. Pour the mixture into champagne glasses.

Top each glass with ginger ale and champagne and drop in a few frozen raspberries. **SERVES 4**

1 cup (250 mL) frozen orange juice concentrate

juice and zest of 1 lemon

1 tsp (5 mL) ground cardamom

1 tsp (5 mL) smoked paprika

2 cups (500 mL) ginger ale

1 bottle sparkling wine

frozen raspberries for garnish

I don't drink often, but recently started mixing drinks for my friends to enjoy. I live in British Columbia and sometimes see bald eagles flying above my house. When I created this recipe, I decided to name it after BC's bald eagles.

Spicy BC Bald Eagle

1½ oz (45 mL) bourbon (I prefer Eagle Rare)

1 Tbsp (15 mL) maple syrup

1 Tbsp (15 mL) crushed basil

1 tsp (5 mL) lime juice

crushed ice

Combine all the ingredients in a shaker and mix well. Pour into a lowball glass. **SERVES 1**

This recipe is inspired by the tamarind water that we bought with gol guppas, *deep-fried, round puff pastries served by Indian street vendors. When I was little, I would go to the vendors for tamarind water on its own. It is spicy and sweet, and has a perfect amount of sourness. I decided to take it one notch higher by giving it a vodka twist.*

Tamarind Tuscan

2 cups (500 mL) tomato juice

½ cup (125 mL) vodka

2 Tbsp (30 mL) tamarind pulp

2 Tbsp (30 mL) crushed mint

1 Tbsp (15 mL) crushed ginger

1 tsp (5 mL) crushed garlic

½ tsp (2 mL) smoked paprika

¼ tsp (1 mL) celery salt

juice of 1 lemon and 1 lime

2 cups (500 mL) ice cubes

Combine all the ingredients in a large shaker and mix well. Serve in lowball glasses. **SERVES 2 TO 4**

I don't drink coffee, and my true indulgence is a homemade chai. It soothes my emotions and completely calms me down after a long, busy day.

Chai

4 cups (1 L) water

10 whole cloves

8 green cardamom pods

4 black cardamom pods

1-inch (2.5 cm) piece ginger

2 Tbsp (30 mL) sugar

2 Tbsp (30 mL) black tea leaves

¾ cup (185 mL) whole milk

In a saucepan, bring the water, spices, sugar and tea to a boil. Turn down the heat to low and simmer for 10 minutes. Pour in the milk and bring to a boil again.

Strain into teacups. **SERVES 4**

After trying a chai latte from a very well-known coffee place, I knew I had to create something better and more affordable. This is for my girlfriends who love chai lattes!

Chai Latte

1 cup (250 mL) milk

1 tsp (5 mL) ground ginger

1 Tbsp (15 mL) sugar

1 Tbsp (15 mL) black tea leaves

⅛ tsp (0.5 mL) ground cloves

¼ tsp (1 mL) ground cardamom

¼ tsp (1 mL) ground cinnamon

In a small pot on medium-high heat, bring the milk, ginger, sugar, black tea leaves and cloves to a simmer. Turn down heat to low and simmer for 10 minutes.

Strain into a 2-cup (500 mL) measure. Using an electric milk frother or espresso machine, steam the chai until it is thick and foamy.

Pour into a large latte cup and spoon foam on top. Sprinkle with cardamom and cinnamon and serve.

SERVES 1

Aaron has a sweet tooth just like his mama. This recipe was created by him, and I am proud of my son for taking a risk and playing with my spices.

Aaron's Hot Chocolate

4 cups (1 L) milk

1 cup (250 mL) heavy (36–40%) cream

3 oz (90 g) good-quality dark chocolate

¼ cup (60 mL) ground cocoa

2 Tbsp (30 mL) sugar

1 tsp (5 mL) ground cardamom

½ tsp (2 mL) ground fennel

pinch of saffron threads

lots of mini marshmallows for topping

In a large saucepan, heat the milk, cream and chocolate on medium-high, whisking frequently, until the chocolate is melted and the liquid is steaming hot.

Pour ¼ cup (60 mL) of the hot milk into a cup and whisk in the rest of the ingredients, except the saffron and marshmallows, until it forms a paste. Whisk the paste into the hot chocolate in the saucepan.

Serve in large mugs, sprinkled with a pinch of saffron and topped with a few marshmallows. **SERVES 4**

Acknowledgements

Thank you to the many partners who helped me through the process of publishing this book: All-Clad, Bernardin, Boos, Cuisinart, Coast Appliances, Denby and Zwilling J.A. Henckels. Hair and makeup for the cover photograph by Suki's Salon.

Index

Page numbers for photographs appear in **boldface**.